NATIVE SHELLS OF AOTEAROA

**ALSO IN THIS SERIES**

*Native Birds of Aotearoa*
*Native Plants of Aotearoa*
*Native Insects of Aotearoa*

# NATIVE SHELLS
# OF AOTEAROA

Bruce Marshall and Kerry Walton

PRESS

# CONTENTS

| | |
|---|---:|
| Introduction | 7 |
| About this book | 14 |
| The shells | 17 |
| Glossary | 128 |
| References | 130 |
| Acknowledgements | 130 |
| Index of species | 131 |
| About the authors | 135 |

# INTRODUCTION

Many people find shells fascinating, and with good reason; they have so many stories to tell about about the creatures that made them, and the environments they lived in.

Aotearoa New Zealand has one of the largest exclusive economic zones in the world. Spanning roughly 30 degrees of latitude (about 3300km), it extends from the subtropical waters surrounding Rangitāhua Kermadec Islands to the subantarctic seas south of Motu Ihupuku Campbell Island. As such, Aotearoa has highly diverse land- and seascapes, and in just about any environment you can imagine you will find molluscs.

The animal kingdom is divided into phyla. Of these, the phylum Mollusca, with approximately 200,000 living species, is the second-most diverse after the Arthropoda (insects, crustaceans, etc.). Most, but not all, mollusc species produce a shell, although not all shells are produced by molluscs. Brachiopods, urchins and barnacles, for example, all produce shells yet belong in different phyla. In this book we focus on some of the frequently encountered shell-producing mollusc species of Aotearoa. Five mollusc classes are commonly encountered:

1. **Chitons (class: Polyplacophora)**, characterised by having eight wing-shaped shells ('valves') embedded within a leathery surrounding girdle. In some species the shells are not visible externally, being completely enveloped by a greatly enlarged girdle. In most chiton species, however, the girdle is of moderate size and shells occupy much of the dorsal surface area.

2. **Bivalves (class: Bivalvia)**, including clams, oysters, mussels, scallops, cockles and others. Most bivalve species have two similar-looking shells that are hinged together, hence the name 'bivalve'. However, some bivalve species have additional valves, and in others the valves have fused together or disappeared entirely at some point in their evolutionary history. Most bivalves are filter-feeders, but many are carnivorous and some are parasites that live attached to other marine species.

3. **Tusk shells (class: Scaphopoda)**, a group of filter-feeding species that live in mud or fine sand. Their tusk-shaped shells were traditionally used to make necklaces or as currency in many indigenous cultures.

4. **Gastropods (class: Gastropoda)**, including slugs, snails, limpets, conchs, nudibranchs and others. Gastropods are the most diverse mollusc class and the only class to occur in terrestrial environments. Most gastropod species live on the sea floor (i.e. they are benthic), while a few are pelagic – living their entire lives among the plankton or floating on the ocean surface. Other gastropod species live on land or in fresh water. Gastropod species have a diverse range of feeding strategies. Many hunt worms or fish with poison darts, others feed on detritus or sessile organisms with their specialised teeth (radulae), and up to a third of marine gastropod species may be parasites. Gastropods have also evolved a diverse range of methods to avoid predation. Some species grow spines, some are poisonous to eat or touch, some grow a thick shell that they can seal with their operculum, while others are well camouflaged. Members of one gastropod family, the carrier shells, go so far as to cement rocks and other shells on to their own shells to blend in with the surrounding sea floor.

5. **Cephalopods (class: Cephalopoda)**, including squids, octopuses, cuttlefish, nautiluses and some less widely known deep-sea groups. Octopuses are among the most intelligent animals: some species can solve puzzles at a level equivalent to that of a human toddler. Many cephalopod species can change their skin colour, or flash with bioluminescence. These adaptations allow them to blend into their environments, ward off a rival, or woo a potential mate.

Molluscs in Aotearoa have been valued by Māori for centuries. Many species were prized as kaimoana (seafood); others were used as tools. Mussel shells, for example, were being used as scrapers to prepare harakeke (flax) for weaving, and the iridescent inner surface of pāua shells was used in fishing lures. Pāua shells were also prized for art, and often formed the eyes in whakairo (carvings). Some mollusc species were used in rongoā (traditional medicine). The shells of many large gastropod species were used as instruments such as flutes or pūtātara (trumpets).

Following the arrival of Europeans in Aotearoa, several mollusc species were taken to Europe by Captain James Cook, the naturalist Joseph Banks and the crew of HMS *Endeavour*. The opal top shell (*Cantharidus opalus*) has the distinction of being the first species unique to Aotearoa (of any type, not just molluscs) to be illustrated and recorded in a scientific journal, in 1774.

A succession of naturalists has since gone on to record approximately 5000 living mollusc species in Aotearoa, 85 percent of which are endemic, meaning that they are found nowhere else. Almost 7000 additional mollusc species are known from the fossil record. New discoveries are being made every year. Continued exploration and advancing genetic technologies are enabling scientists to probe ever deeper into mollusc diversity and the relationships between species. About half of all known mollusc species from Aotearoa are yet to receive a scientific name.

In terrestrial environments, a handful of leaf litter from any forest in Aotearoa is likely to contain anywhere between ten and forty land-snail species – an unusually high diversity for a temperate region. Most land-snail species are tiny: some do not exceed 1mm at maturity. Many species have never been seen alive, as they may live in seldom-searched regions or habitats, such as under leaves high in the forest canopy. Others live on the forest floor, such as the endangered and protected giant *Powelliphanta* land snails, which can grow up to 90mm across and weigh more than a tūī.

Many large land-snail species are endangered as the result of historical over-collecting, habitat loss and the introduction of predators such as pigs, thrushes, hedgehogs, possums and rats. In addition to alarming predation rates, climate change is causing some regions to become drier. Browsing by introduced herbivores can trample snails and reduce undergrowth cover, which can further dry out the forest floor, making it easier for predators like rodents and weka to locate snails.

Marine environments are often under stress, too. Bottom-trawling by fishing boats crushes animals and smothers them with plumes of disturbed sediment. Land-use modification can also result in sedimentation in coastal regions. Without lace-coral, bivalve and sponge beds providing some three-dimensional structures on which to grow and shelter, the larvae of many sand- and mud-dwelling mollusc species cannot survive.

Other threats to marine molluscs include marine pollutants, which can render mollusc populations infertile or directly result in deaths. Global shipping traffic brings with it the risk of introduction of invasive species, which can displace or destroy native species. Finally, as the climate changes, marine heatwaves are increasing in frequency, displacing those species that are unable to adapt to abnormal temperatures or affecting the balance of predator and prey species in an environment.

Submarine volcanoes and hydrothermal vents are rich in precious metals, but seafloor mining threatens the unique marine communities that call these places home. Too deep to receive much sunlight, hydrothermal vent communities produce energy not from photosynthesis but from chemosynthesis, a process whereby bacteria produce sugars through metabolism of hydrogen sulphide or methane. In Aotearoa, many hydrothermal vents are spread along the Kermadec Ridge; at many of these sites there are dense beds of giant mussels and other mollusc species that occur nowhere else.

Many mollusc species are of great significance in the fisheries and aquaculture sectors. Oysters and mussels are two of the three most profitable aquaculture species in Aotearoa (the third is salmon); together they contribute hundreds of millions of dollars to annual GDP. Other mollusc species can be found in limited or experimental aquaculture fisheries. Wild-caught fisheries exist for a range of species, including cockles, tuatua, surf clams, mussels, scallops, oysters, pāua and squid. All kaimoana species have restrictions on the size and/or number of individuals that one person may collect, and these restrictions can vary between regions.

Bivalve populations are highly susceptible to waves of disease. The recently introduced oyster disease *Bonamia*, for example, is intermittently spreading through the oyster beds of Te Ara a Kiwa Foveaux Strait and threatening nearby oyster farms. When you encounter a large wash-up of bivalves on a beach, the chances are that they were weakened or killed by a disease rather than by storm action alone. It is advised not to gather shellfish that are washed up, found near ports, or during blooms of toxin-producing algae; filter-feeding bivalves often accumulate toxins and pollutants from the water in their tissues.

Shell collecting is a popular pastime in Aotearoa. It is irresistible to many of us to keep trinkets that we encounter on our travels. Some collectors may limit themselves to a few large specimens displayed on a mantelpiece, while others keep drawers full of shells with each specimen carefully labelled and sorted by species. Shell exhibitions take place every few years and can attract hundreds of visitors. Three shell clubs are presently active in Aotearoa, located in Auckland, Wellington and Whangārei. Contacting a shell club can be a good way to learn more about local collecting spots, to expand one's collection, or to have specimens identified. Several websites and books offer other means of identifying specimens.

People are encouraged to be mindful of local collecting restrictions. All large land-snail species (and a few of the small ones) are covered by the Wildlife Act, making the collection or possession of their empty shells illegal. Rāhui, marine reserves, national parks and other forms of protection can also prohibit the collection of shells.

Reporting discoveries and donating specimens to research institutions such as Te Papa can assist mollusc research, conservation and biosecurity efforts. Other means of contributing include the documentation of finds through citizen science social media platforms like iNaturalist. Records of the habitat, behaviour, location, date and time of day for an observation all contribute to our collective ecological knowledge of a species.

Scientists are always looking to detect and monitor the spread of invasive species, or species' changing distributions, habitats and behaviours. One of the most abundant and widespread invasive species on Earth originated from Aotearoa – the humble freshwater snail *Potamopyrgus antipodarum*.

All species require several environmental conditions (their 'niche') to be met in order to survive and persist. The combination of these conditions differs between species. As an example, it may be said that a species is 'found throughout Te Waipounamu South Island', when it may in fact be restricted to muddy estuaries or a certain forest type and absent from the many other habitat types around the island. Species' distributions may also be influenced by those of their predator, competitor, prey or host species. Addionally, some species are present in a region only at certain times of the year, or in some years but not others.

The dispersal potential of a species plays a significant role in determining its distributions. Does the species have a larval form that drifts with the ocean currents? Might this species attach to the hulls of ships or the holdfasts of kelp and be moved great distances? The geography and geological history of a region also shapes the distributions of species as they can present a range of physical and physiological barriers to the dispersal of species. Areas where there is suitable habitat today could have been very different during the last glacial maximum, thousands of years ago, when conditions were much cooler and sea levels were over 100 metres lower than at present. As they result from numerous complex drivers, contemporary species' distributions are often quite nuanced and how they came about can be poorly understood.

## MOLLUSC COLLECTIONS AT TE PAPA

Te Papa holds by far the largest mollusc collection in Aotearoa, with roughly 500,000 collection lots (a lot refers to all of the specimens of one species collected at the same place at the same time) and totalling several million specimens of molluscs from all around the world. The collection arose from donations of private collections as well as sampling efforts by successive museum staff and other researchers. Collections staff partner with iwi and other research institutions to supplement the collection with records of species, forms or localities that are less well represented.

Large natural history collections in institutions like Te Papa are an invaluable tool enabling researchers to distinguish between very similar-looking species, as well as between different life-stages of each species, to establish what species occur in each region, and to suggest or reveal how the fauna of a site may respond to various pressures such as pollution, climate change, invasive species and fishing.

The colossal squid from Antarctica is Te Papa's most popular public exhibit. However, only a small proportion of Te Papa's collection is on display. The remainder is used primarily for research, cultural or reference purposes. These collections allow researchers and community members to connect with rare or extinct species and populations of native species. Samples are lent to scientists throughout Aotearoa and across the world for scientific research to further improve our understanding of mollusc diversity. Specimens from the collections have featured on New Zealand Post stamps as well as in various publications and art projects.

Te Papa's scientists have been partnering with the University of Otago to pioneer genetic techniques that enable researchers to sequence DNA from shells that are thousands of years old; this makes most of the non-fossil specimens in the collection available for some aspects of genetic research. By looking at the genetic code from prehistoric and historical records, researchers can see how successive waves of human arrival, together with the species we have introduced, have affected the fauna of Aotearoa.

Due to these technological advances and extensive historical collecting efforts, there is sometimes less need to collect fresh samples, which can be difficult, expensive and/or unethical if the species are endangered or live in remote or vulnerable environments. Many mollusc species are only known from their shells as they have never been seen or collected alive. That most mollusc species produce a shell with moderate preservation potential is one of the reasons why they are a great group to use for understanding biodiversity patterns.

Other mollusc research projects at Te Papa have examined fauna living and feeding on a variety of unusual habitats in the deep sea, including decaying wood and algae, and fish and whale remains, including decaying flesh, bones and baleen.

Te Papa staff provide advice to the Department of Conservation and iwi on endangered species, and to the Ministry for Primary Industries and other agencies with regard to biosecurity threats. With congruent climate and conservation crises, and limited research or conservation funding, ongoing mollusc research is critical to properly understanding and effectively protecting the unique species and habitats of Aotearoa.

*Bruce Marshall, Kerry Walton*

# ABOUT THIS BOOK

This book was inspired by a succession of small nature guides on the flora and fauna of Aotearoa New Zealand published in the 1950s and 1960s. The classic guide *Native Shells* (1955), written by former Te Papa curator RK Dell as part of the *Nature in New Zealand* series published by AH & AW Reed, was a source for stylistic inspiration. The majority of the images were digitally stylised from high-resolution photographs of Te Papa specimens by Dr Jean-Claude Stahl.

In addition to scientific (Latin) names, vernacular (also termed 'common') te reo Māori and/or English names are given for each species. There are many additional vernacular names that we have either overlooked or omitted, for simplicity or out of concern for misapplying them. Te reo names were sourced from *The New Zealand Seashore Guide* (2022) and *New Zealand Coastal Marine Invertebrates* (2010).

Often, vernacular names apply to more than one species (e.g. scallop and tuatua), or to one of several forms or parts of a species (e.g. paper nautilus, which refers only to the shells produced by the females of a genus of octopus; or kōwhā, which refers specifically to the meat of cockles). To reduce the risk of such confusion, scientific names are governed by a strict set of rules. Even so, scientific names sometimes change as relationships between species and populations become better understood.

The species' distributions reported in this book are greatly generalised and simplified. Aotearoa has more than 700 offshore islands. For brevity, where reporting species' distributions, this book refers to the main islands and offshore islands only, including the following groupings:

- **Both main islands** – coasts of Te Ika-a-Māui North Island and Te Waipounamu South Island

- **Three main islands** – as above including Rakiura Stewart Island

- **Subantarctic islands** – Tini Heke Snares Islands, Motu Maha Auckland Islands, Motu Ihupuku Campbell Island, Moutere Hauriri Bounty Islands and Motu Mahue Antipodes Islands

This book includes 161 shell-producing mollusc species, representing about sixty-seven different families. Many microscopic or deep-water species are more abundant than the species depicted here, but those seldom come to the attention of the public. While far from comprehensive, given the vast number of mollusc species in this country, this book aims to give the reader an appreciation of the diversity and beauty of molluscs in Aotearoa.

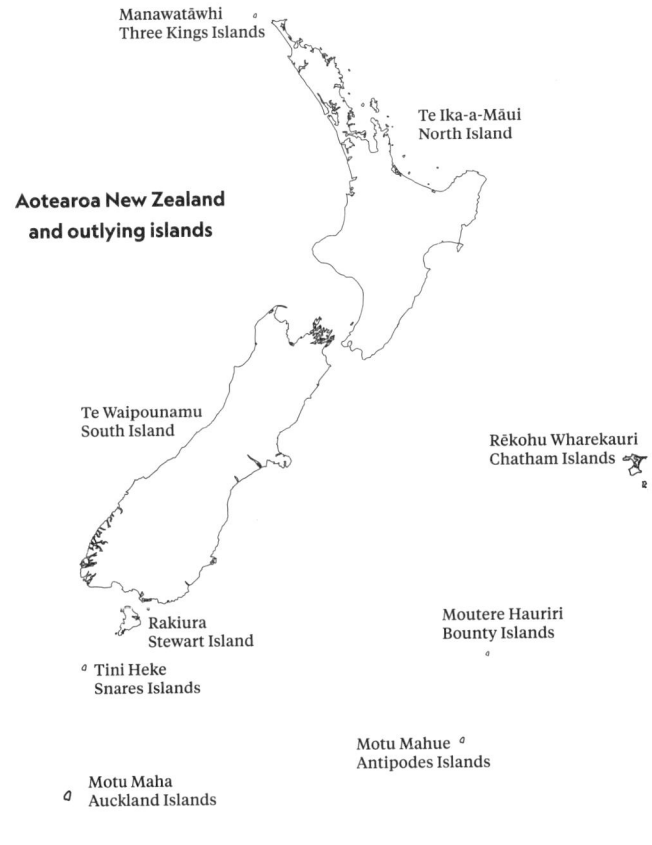

# THE SHELLS

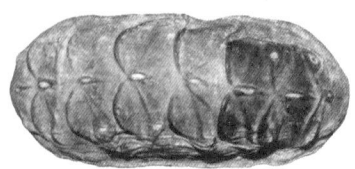

**PAPATUA**
## SNAKESKIN CHITON
*Sypharochiton pelliserpentis*

**Distribution:** Three main islands; Rēkohu Wharekauri Chatham Islands; also south-eastern Australia. Lives intertidally, on rocks and shell.

**Size:** Total length to 42mm.

One of the most common chitons, found on hard substrates in estuaries and rocky coasts. The English common name derives from the large scales on the girdle, which resemble those of a snake. A very similar species, *Sypharochiton sinclairi*, differs in having a bluish ring on the girdle. Snakeskin chitons can be distinguished from green chitons by the presence of regular colour bands on their girdle.

**PAPATUA**
## GREEN CHITON
*Chiton glaucus*

**Distribution:** Three main islands; also introduced to Tasmania. Lives intertidally and in shallow sublittoral, on rocks and shell.

**Size:** Total length to 55mm.

Common on rocky shorelines around Aotearoa New Zealand, these range in colour from vivid greens to shades of blue-grey, orange and brown. While normally without a pattern, many juvenile and some adult green chitons can have coloured lines and blotches on the dorsal surface of their shells. The similar species *Ischnochiton maorianus* and *Onithochiton neglectus* differ in being more elongate and in having raised hair-like girdle scales, respectively.

**KAOKAOROA, PAPATUA**
## BUTTERFLY CHITON
*Cryptoconchus porosus*

**Distribution:** Three main islands; Rēkohu Wharekauri Chatham Islands. Lives intertidally and in shallow sublittoral, on rocks and shell.

**Size:** Total length to 73mm.

Unlike most chiton species, the shells of butterfly chitons are covered by soft tissue. The English name arose because each of the bluish-white internal shells resembles a butterfly. Butterfly chitons can be shades of red, orange and brown, and are often found in low-tide rockpools among sponges and algae.

### KUTE
# RAZOR MUSSEL
*Solemya parkinsonii*

**Distribution:** Three main islands; Rēkohu Wharekauri Chatham Islands. Lives intertidally to 376m deep, in mud and sand.

**Size:** Shell length to 83mm.

This mussel lives deep in the sediment where there is very little oxygen. It feeds through a symbiotic relationship with bacteria that metabolise hydrogen sulphide – the same gas that gives Rotorua and many estuaries their unique smell. The delicate frills that ring beach-cast razor mussel shells are highly distinctive.

### HOEMOANA, HURUROA, KŪKUKU, KŪKUKUROA, KUKUPATI, KUPA, KŪPĀ, PATI, PATIKUKU, TORETORE, WAHAROA
# HORSE MUSSEL, NEW ZEALAND PEN SHELL
*Atrina zelandica*

**Distribution:** Three main islands; Rēkohu Wharekauri Chatham Islands. Lives intertidally to 103m deep, partially buried in sand or mud.

**Size:** Shell length to 447mm.

Horse mussels produce Aotearoa New Zealand's largest shells. They can form moderately dense beds that stabilise the sea floor and provide a safe habitat for juvenile fish and benthic invertebrate species that cannot survive on loose sand. Rows of spines help to keep the mussel in place within the sediment. Their beds are especially vulnerable to dredging. In some regions, they are considered kaimoana.

### TŪRORO
# ARK SHELL
*Barbatia novaezelandiae*

**Distribution:** Three main islands; Rēkohu Wharekauri Chatham Islands, Tini Heke Snares Islands. Lives intertidally to 256m deep, attached by byssal threads to rocks and other hard substrates.

**Size:** Shell length to 79mm.

The long and finely sculptured hinge of ark shells is highly distinctive among living bivalves. When living or freshly dead, ark shells are covered with dark hairs. Smaller relatives of the ark shell can be found in shallow water in northern Aotearoa.

**KUKU, PŌROHE, TAORE, TORETORE, TORITORI**

# BLUE MUSSEL

*Mytilus planulatus*

**Distribution:** Three main islands; Rēkohu Wharekauri Chatham Islands, Rangitāhua Kermadec Islands, Motu Maha Auckland Islands, Motu Ihupuku Campbell Island. Also south-eastern Australia. Lives intertidally to a few metres deep, attached to hard substrates.

**Size:** Shell height to 150mm.

The number of blue mussel species worldwide, and what Latin names to use for them all, remain unresolved. Blue mussels from the subantarctic islands grow much larger than mainland individuals, which seldom exceed 70mm. While a popular seafood in much of the world, the green-lipped mussel is preferred in Aotearoa New Zealand.

**KUKU, KŪTAI, PŌROHE**

# GREEN-LIPPED MUSSEL

*Perna canaliculus*

**Distribution:** Three main islands; Rēkohu Wharekauri Chatham Islands. Lives intertidally and in shallow sublittoral, attached to hard substrates.

**Size:** Shell length to 230mm.

Marketed as the New Zealand Greenshell mussel, this is a significant wild-caught seafood and aquaculture species. Mussels generally reach a harvestable size at between four and six years of age, depending on food availability. Pea crabs are often encountered dwelling inside living mussels' shells.

**KŪTAI, PUKANIKANI, PŪKANIKANI**

# RIBBED MUSSEL

*Aulacomya maoriana*

**Distribution:** Three main islands (south-eastern Te Ika-a-Māui North Island); subantarctic islands. Lives intertidally and in shallow sublittoral, attached to hard substrates.

**Size:** Shell length to 115mm.

This species is similar to the blue mussel, with which it often lives, but distinguished by numerous fine ribs running the length of the shell. Juvenile ribbed mussels tend to be a light or golden brown, while larger shells may be purplish or brown.

#### HĀNEA, KUKUPARA, NIANIA
# BLACK MUSSEL
*Xenostrobus neozelanicus*

**Distribution:** Three main islands; Tini Heke Snares Islands, Motu Maha Auckland Islands. Lives intertidally and in immediate sublittoral, attached to hard substrates.

**Size:** Shell length to 34mm.

This mussel can can often be seen densely coating exposed rocks at mid- to high tide. A similar species, *X. securis*, grows larger, has a brown or black shell, and generally lives in more brackish habitats such as in tidal river mouths.

#### PUREWHA
# BROWN MUSSEL
*Modiolus areolatus*

**Distribution:** Three main islands; Rēkohu Wharekauri Chatham Islands, subantarctic islands; also southern Australia. Lives intertidally to 446m deep, attached to hard substrates.

**Size:** Shell length to 120mm.

The brown mussel is easily identified by its distinctive shell shape, which includes a flared flange near the beak. The outer shell layer is lined with fine hairs. Specimens can exceed 100mm in the subantarctic islands, but they seldom grow as large on the mainland.

#### KORONA, KUKU-MAU-TOKA
# NESTING MUSSEL
*Musculus impactus*

**Distribution:** Three main islands; Rēkohu Wharekauri Chatham Islands; also Australia. Lives intertidally to 59m deep, attached to rocks or other invertebrates on soft sediments.

**Size:** Shell length to 48mm.

Nesting mussels are so-named because they build woven brown filamentous 'nests' that fully enclose the shell when living – resembling the cocoon of the gum emperor moth. They often live in clusters attached to rocks or shell debris. Their shells range in colour from greys and browns in mature individuals to vivid lime-greens in younger individuals.

**KUA KUA, KUHAKUHA**

# LARGE DOG COCKLE

*Tucetona laticostata*

**Distribution:** Three main islands (off Te Rerenga Wairua Cape Reinga and eastern Te Ika-a-Māui North Island, northern and southern Te Waipounamu South Island); Rēkohu Wharekauri Chatham Islands, Tini Heke Snares Islands. Lives 8–153m deep, in soft sediment.

**Size:** Shell height to 124mm.

These cockles have very thick and heavy shells; some can resemble a cricket ball in terms of size, shape, colour and weight. Dog cockles have a distinctive elongate and near-symmetrical hinge comprising many fine striations. Their shells often contain sponge and bryozoan species that bore into the thick shell.

# SMALL DOG COCKLE

*Glycymeris modesta*

**Distribution:** Three main islands (off Te Rerenga Wairua Cape Reinga, north-eastern and south-western Te Ika-a-Māui North Island, northern and southern Te Waipounamu South Island); Rēkohu Wharekauri Chatham Islands. Lives at 2–49m deep, in soft sediment.

**Size:** Shell length to 31mm.

This cockle has a variable and often brightly patterned shell with a soft, hairy outer shell layer. The shell has a much smoother and glossier surface than large dog cockles of a similar size; both species have a distinctive elongate and near-symmetrical hinge that distinguishes them from most other bivalves.

# NUT SHELL

*Linucula hartvigiana*

**Distribution:** Both main islands (southern Te Waipounamu South Island). Lives intertidally to 4m deep, in mud and muddy sand.

**Size:** Shell length to 11mm.

These can be extremely common in estuarine environments. They have a distinctive hinge comprising many rows of sharp, interlocking teeth. Several similar species can be found in different habitats and regions around Aotearoa New Zealand. The concave inner surface of the nut shell is silvery and iridescent.

## GREEN WINDOW OYSTER
*Monia zelandica*

**Distribution:** Three main islands; Rēkohu Wharekauri Chatham Islands; three western subantarctic islands; also southern Australia. Lives intertidally to 183m deep, attached to hard substrates.

**Size:** Shell diameter to 77mm.

Window oysters (superfamily Anomioidea) in Aotearoa New Zealand can be distinguished from true oysters (family Ostreidae) by the presence of a large circular opening in the valve that adheres to the substrate. Generally cream or olive in colour, the green window oyster has a distinctive green area on the inner surface of the shell. Window oysters get their name from a large near-transparent tropical species that was traditionally used as a glass substitute in windows and ornaments.

### PORO
## GOLDEN JINGLE SHELL, YELLOW WINDOW OYSTER
*Anomia trigonopsis*

**Distribution:** Te Ika-a-Māui North Island; also south-eastern Australia. Lives intertidally to 165m deep, attached to rocks and other shells.

**Size:** Shell diameter to 82mm.

This species is commonly encountered on beaches in northern Te Ika-a-Māui North Island. Their shells are thin but surprisingly strong, and range in colour from cream to yellow to golden orange. Divers looking for scallops often find yellow window oysters that have taken on the wavy shape of the scallop shells they have settled on.

### PAKIRA, PUKIRA
## BOX SHELL, COMMON MYADORA
*Myadora striata*

**Distribution:** Three main islands. Lives intertidally to 23m deep, in soft sediment.

**Size:** Shell length to 47mm.

This species has an unusually shaped shell comprising a near-flattened valve and an inflated valve. Between the beak and the shell margin that sticks out of the sediment is a distinctive concave surface. The inside of the shell has a silvery lustre.

**KARAURIA, NGĀKIHI, REPE, TIO, TIO POHATU, TIO REPE,
TIO REPEREPE, TIOKOHATU, TIOPARA, TIOREPE**

# ROCK OYSTER

*Saccostrea glomerata*

**Distribution:** Northern Te Ika-a-Māui North Island as far south as Aotea Harbour on the west coast and Te Whakatōhea Ōhiwa Harbour on the east coast; Rēkohu Wharekauri Chatham Islands; also south-eastern Australia. Lives intertidally, attached to hard substrates.

**Size:** Shell length to 109mm.

This species has a jagged and wavy shell margin. Their shells are a pale grey trending to purple on the margins. A series of fine crenulations inside the shell, along the margins near the hinge, distinguish this species from the Pacific oyster.

**TIO, TIO PARA, TIO PARUPARU, TIOPARA, TIOREPE**

# BLUFF OYSTER, DREDGE OYSTER, FLAT OYSTER

*Ostrea chilensis*

**Distribution:** Three main islands; Rēkohu Wharekauri Chatham Islands; also Chile. Lives intertidally to 293m deep, on hard substrates; adults also live on soft substrates where hard surfaces like dead shells are present for larvae to settle on.

**Size:** Shell length to 108mm.

Said by many to be one of the best-tasting oysters in the world, the dredge fishery for this species is threatened by the disease *Bonamia*. This oyster differs from rock and Pacific oysters in having greenish patches on the interior surface of the shell rather than being predominantly purple.

**TIO**

# PACIFIC OYSTER

*Magallana gigas*

**Distribution:** Te Ika-a-Māui North Island and north-western and south-eastern Te Waipounamu South Island; also the Atlantic, Mediterranean and Indo-Pacific. Lives intertidally and in immediate sublittoral, on hard substrates.

**Size:** Shell length to 242mm.

During recent decades Pacific oysters have become common and widespread around much of Aotearoa New Zealand. They form a significant aquaculture industry as they grow larger and faster than the very similar native rock oyster.

**KUAKUA, TIPA, TIPAI, TUPA**
# NEW ZEALAND SCALLOP, QUEEN SCALLOP
*Pecten novaezelandiae*

**Distribution:** Three main islands (northern and southern Te Waipounamu); Rēkohu Wharekauri Chatham Islands. Lives at low-tide level to 121m deep, on soft substrates.

**Size:** Shell diameter to 174mm.

This species has great cultural and commercial significance in Aotearoa New Zealand. Unfortunately, overfishing and habitat degradation have contributed to the collapse of queen scallop fisheries in most regions. Scallops have hundreds of eyes, each sitting on a small eye stalk lining the inner shell margins. They are surprisingly capable swimmers, moving by rapidly closing their valves and expelling water.

**TIPA**
# COMMON FAN SCALLOP
*Talochlamys zelandiae*

**Distribution:** Three main islands; Rēkohu Wharekauri Chatham Islands, Tini Heke Snares Islands, Motu Maha Auckland Islands. Lives intertidally to 549m deep, attached to hard substrates.

**Size:** Shell length to 58mm.

The spiny shells of these scallops are often covered by sponges, providing effective camouflage. Fan scallop shells vary significantly in colour. They are usually purple, orange or a mixture of both colours. Red or white shells are less common, and pure yellow shells are quite rare and highly sought-after by shell collectors.

# FINE FAN SCALLOP
*Talochlamys gemmulata*

**Distribution:** Three main islands; Rēkohu Wharekauri Chatham Islands, Tini Heke Snares Islands. Lives at 20–293m deep, attached to rocks or shells.

**Size:** Shell length to 73mm.

This species has a much more finely sculptured shell than the common fan scallop. Shells grow larger in cooler waters. They tend to be either dark purple or bright orange in colour, but come in a wide range of colours and patterns.

#### PŪRIMU
# PURPLE COCKLE
*Purpurocardia purpurata*

**Distribution:** Three main islands (west of Te Rerenga Wairua Cape Reinga, north-eastern and south-western Te Ika-a-Māui North Island); Rēkohu Wharekauri Chatham Islands, Motu Maha Auckland Islands. Lives at 5–293m deep, in soft sediments.

**Size:** Shell length to 45mm.

The thick and heavy shell of this species is whitish externally, commonly with a brownish colour pattern, and typically has purplish patches within. A second, rarer, species is more elongate but seldom washes ashore except in northern Te Ika-a-Māui North Island.

# LACE COCKLE
*Divalucina cumingi*

**Distribution:** Three main islands; Rēkohu Wharekauri Chatham Islands; also Australia. Lives in immediate sublittoral to 8m deep, in soft sediments.

**Size:** Shell length to 45mm.

This is a highly distinctive, almost circular species, with intricate chevron patterns on its shell resembling fine lace embroidery. Empty shells are commonly encountered on sandy beaches around Aotearoa New Zealand. Members of the lace cockle family (Lucinidae) are chemosymbiotic; they are rarely seen alive because they live deeply buried in sediment where hydrogen sulphide levels are higher.

#### ANGARITE, KĀKAHI, KŌKOTA, KOTAKOTA, NGAINGAI, PIPI, TAI AWA, TAIAWA
# PIPI
*Paphies australis*

**Distribution:** Three main islands; Rēkohu Wharekauri Chatham Islands, Motu Maha Auckland Islands. Lives intertidally and in immediate sublittoral, in sand and muddy sand.

**Size:** Shell length to 95mm.

The pipi is an important kaimoana species in Aotearoa, normally found on relatively sheltered sandy beaches. Pipi generally differ from tuatua species in having a more symmetrical shell with more-rounded margins. Their shells are cream, grey or white, with a thin, light brown periostracum.

**MOEONE, ROROA, TAIWHATIWHATI,
TOHEROA, TUPEHOKURA**
# TOHEROA
*Paphies ventricosa*

**Distribution:** Northern and south-western Te Ika-a-Māui North Island, and north-western and southern Te Waipounamu South Island. Lives intertidally, in sand.

**Size:** Shell length to 169mm.

A culturally significant kaimoana species, toheroa were once harvested in large numbers. A combination of overfishing, vehicles driving on beaches (which can crush the animals that live at the mid-tide level) and possibly the drainage of coastal soils for agriculture have contributed to significant declines in toheroa numbers and the closure of the fishery except for limited customary harvests.

**KAHITUA, KAITUA, PIPI TAIRAKI, PIPI-TAIRAKI,
TAIRAKI, TAIWHATIWHATI, TUA, TUATUA**
# TUATUA
*Paphies subtriangulata*

**Distribution:** Three main islands; Rēkohu Wharekauri Chatham Islands, Motu Maha Auckland Islands. Lives at low-tide level in sand.

**Size:** Shell length to 99mm.

Tuatua and southern tuatua co-occur throughout much of their distributions and can be extremely difficult to distinguish. In general, the tuatua has a more triangular shell, with a straighter long-edge. The shell of the tuatua is typically greyish white, whereas that of the southern tuatua typically has a yellowish hue.

**TUATUA**
# SOUTHERN TUATUA
*Paphies donacina*

**Distribution:** Three main islands. Lives at 2–4m deep, in sand.

**Size:** Shell length to 105mm.

The southern tuatua is frequently confused with toheroa and tuatua. While the shells of tuatua lie flat when pressed against a flat surface, an equivalent-sized toheroa shell will wobble on an axis. See above for distinction from tuatua.

**HANIKURA, HANIKURA-PATU**
# LARGE WEDGE SHELL
*Macomona liliana*

**Distribution:** Three main islands. Lives intertidally, in mud and sand.

**Size:** Shell length to 81mm.

This species lives in harbours and sheltered bays, where it is a filter-feeder. They grow largest in larger harbours and sandier environments, but do not generally live on open coasts.

# ANGLED WEDGE SHELL, BUTTERFLY SHELL
*Bartschicoma gaimardi*

**Distribution:** Both main islands. Lives in shallow sublittoral in soft sediment.

**Size:** Shell length to 75mm.

The angled wedge shell resembles the large wedge shell, from which it differs in having a thinner, less inflated and more elongate shell. It lives on sandy coasts.

# ROUND WEDGE SHELL
*Pseudarcopagia disculus*

**Distribution:** Three main islands; Rēkohu Wharekauri Chatham Islands, Tini Heke Snares Islands. Lives intertidally and in shallow sublittoral, in sand and gravel among rocky reefs.

**Size:** Shell length to 39mm.

This species has a distinctive yellow patch inside the shell near the beak. It is the smallest and most rounded of the common wedge shells, and has a sculpture of fine concentric ribs.

**KAIKAIKARORO**
# TRIANGLE SHELL
*Crassula aequilatera*

**Distribution:** Three main islands. Lives at 3–8m deep, in sand.

**Size:** Shell length to 75mm.

This is one of the most ubiquitous mollusc species in Aotearoa New Zealand. Their shells are commonly washed up on surf beaches around the country. They differ from the trough shells in having much more sharply angled edges. Young triangle shells are purple or pink; the shells become pale as the animal grows larger.

# LARGE TROUGH SHELL
*Mactra murchisoni*

**Distribution:** Both main islands (northern and southern Te Waipounamu South Island). Lives at 4–8m deep, in sand.

**Size:** Shell length to 102mm.

The large trough shell lives on exposed surf beaches, where it lies buried in the sediments where the waves break. Fresh shells are near-white, with a thin brown periostracum; old shells are often stained black by the sediment.

# TROUGH SHELL
*Mactra discors*

**Distribution:** North-eastern and southern Te Ika-a-Māui North Island, and northern and southern Te Waipounamu South Island. Lives at 3–7m deep, in sand.

**Size:** Shell length to 92mm.

This species differs from the less common large trough shell in having a slightly more evenly rounded shell margin and in attaining a smaller size. However, the two species can be quite difficult to distinguish. A less common and far smaller species, *Maorimactra ordinaria*, resembles juvenile trough shells but is far more angular.

### ROROA
## LANCE MACTRA
*Resania lanceolata*

**Distribution:** Both main islands (Te Waipounamu South Island as far south as Warrington). Lives at 2–4m deep, in soft sediments.

**Size:** Shell length to 120mm.

The lance mactra has a thin, delicate shell that is usually white or grey with a golden-brown periostracum. Despite living in shallow water, they are active burrowers and usually only wash ashore after storms.

### PERARO, PIPI ROA
## SCIMITAR MACTRA
*Zenatia acinaces*

**Distribution:** Three main islands. Lives at 6–49m deep, in soft sediments.

**Size:** Shell length to 118mm.

This species superficially resembles the lance mactra in being elongate with a grey or white shell and a golden-brown periostracum. However, both ends of the scimitar mactra are quite rounded, while the end of the lance mactra that faces down into the sediment is more sharply angled.

## DEEP BURROWER, GEODUCK, NEW ZEALAND GOOEY DUCK
*Panopea zelandica*

**Distribution:** Three main islands (northern and south-western Te Ika-a-Māui North Island, northern Te Waipounamu South Island). Lives at 5–25m deep, in soft sediment.

**Size:** Shell length to 149mm.

The deep burrower has an extremely long siphon, which enables the shell to be buried deep within the sediment, reducing the risk of predation or disinterment during storms. A limited scuba-based commercial harvest at Mohua Golden Bay uses water jets to liquify the sand around the animal to make it easier to extract. Foreign gooey duck species live for many decades. It remains to be seen how sustainable the labour-intensive fishery will prove.

**TUANGI HARURU**
# COARSE BISCUIT CLAM, COARSE DOSINIA
*Dosinia anus*

**Distribution:** Three main islands. Lives at low-tide level to 10m deep, in sand.

**Size:** Shell length to 83mm.

This species has an orange shell with a white to purple interior. Beached shells frequently fade to white. They live on surf beaches and are often washed ashore in their thousands after a storm.

**HAHARI, HĀKARI, HARIHARI**
# FINE BISCUIT CLAM, FINE DOSINIA
*Dosinia subrosea*

**Distribution:** Three main islands. Lives at 5–10m deep, in sand.

**Size:** Shell length to 75mm.

The fine dosinia is usually smaller than the coarse dosinia and has a smoother shell – most notably near the shell margins. White individuals are common, although most fine dosinia are a pale orange, with white to purple inside the shell.

# SMALL DOSINIA
*Dosinia maoriana*

**Distribution:** Northern and south-western Te Ika-a-Māui North Island; Rēkohu Wharekauri Chatham Islands. Lives at low-tide level to 59m deep, in soft sediment.

**Size:** Shell length to 47mm.

This white-shelled small dosinia is easily mistaken for a juvenile of one of the larger *Dosinia* species. Another pale and similarly sized species, *Dosinia lambata*, differs in having very fine sculpture.

## LARGE VENUS SHELL

*Dosina mactracea*

**Distribution:** Three main islands; Rēkohu Wharekauri Chatham Islands, Motu Maha Auckland Islands. Lives intertidally to 139m deep, in soft sediment.

**Size:** Shell length to 71mm.

Immature individuals of this species have bands of reddish-brown blotches extending from the beak. However, these are absent from mature individuals, which are cream in colour. Their shells are often stained orange or brown with metal precipitate or black by anaerobic mud.

### TĀWERA
## MORNING STAR

*Tawera spissa*

**Distribution:** Three main islands; Rēkohu Wharekauri Chatham Islands, Chatham Rise, Motu Maha Auckland Islands. Lives at low-tide level to 139m deep, in sand.

**Size:** Shell length to 34mm.

The morning star is one of the most common shallow-water molluscs in Aotearoa New Zealand. Their shells are either cream or brown, and they are often intricately patterned with bands or wavy lines. Morning star shells form dense beds that provide food and habitat for a range of other species.

### HINANGI, HŪAI, HUANGI, HŪANGIANGI, HŪNGUNGI, HŪWAI, KŌWHĀ, PIPI, TANETANE, TUAKI, TUANGI, TUNGANGI
## COCKLE

*Austrovenus stutchburyi*

**Distribution:** Three main islands; Rēkohu Wharekauri Chatham Islands, Motu Maha Auckland Islands. Lives intertidally, in mud and muddy sand.

**Size:** Shell length to 80mm.

This important kaimoana species is common in harbours, estuaries and sheltered bays all around Aotearoa. Cockles are often infected by a parasite that reduces their ability to bury themselves, rendering them more vulnerable to predation by seabirds, which serve as an intermediary host for the parasite.

### PŪKAURI
## FRILLED VENUS SHELL
*Bassina yatei*

**Distribution:** Three main islands (northern and eastern Te Waipounamu South Island). Lives at 6–9m deep, in soft sediment.

**Size:** Shell length to 67mm.

The frilled venus shell can be pale or a buttery yellow colour, with purple near the beak. The delicate frills help to secure the shell in the sediment, but these are usually worn down on beached specimens.

### KAIKAIKARORO, KARORO, TUAKI, TUANGI
## RIBBED VENUS SHELL
*Leukoma crassicosta*

**Distribution:** Three main islands; Rēkohu Wharekauri Chatham Islands. Lives intertidally and in immediate sublittoral, in sand and gravel among rocky reefs.

**Size:** Shell length to 61mm.

This species lives in the same unusual habitat for a filter-feeding bivalve as the round wedge shell (see page 39). Their shells are usually white but can be cream in colour.

### HAHARI, HĀKARI, HARIHARI
## OBLONG VENUS SHELL
*Venerupis largillierti*

**Distribution:** Three main islands; Rēkohu Wharekauri Chatham Islands, Motu Maha Auckland Islands, Motu Ihupuku Campbell Island. Lives intertidally to 6m deep, in soft sediment.

**Size:** Shell length to 75mm.

This species resembles the ribbed venus in size and shape but differs in having a far finer sculpture. Young individuals are often brightly patterned with brown lines and blotches, but mature individuals are pale.

## ELEGANT VENUS SHELL

*Irus elegans*

**Distribution:** Both main islands (eastern Te Waipounamu South Island). Lives intertidally, embedded within soft rock.

**Size:** Shell length to 60mm.

This species lives embedded in soft rock platforms in the same environment as the true rock borers (family Pholadidae). The elegant venus is quite consistently shaped, with a series of thin frills near the shell margin.

## ROUGH VENUS SHELL

*Irus reflexus*

**Distribution:** Three main islands; Rēkohu Wharekauri Chatham Islands. Lives intertidally, on hard substrates.

**Size:** Shell length to 29mm.

This species closely resembles the elegant venus, but is generally smaller and less elongate. The rough venus lives in crevices and its shape is often twisted and irregular, matching the cavity it has settled within.

## PURPLE SUNSET SHELL

*Hiatula nitida*

**Distribution:** Both main islands; Rēkohu Wharekauri Chatham Islands. Lives at low-tide level and in shallow sublittoral in sand.

**Size:** Shell length to 55mm.

This is a delicate and brightly coloured species. The carbonate part of the shell is a lavender-purple while the periostracum is olive-green. A similar species, *Hiatula siliquens*, differs subtly in shell shape, being more rounded and, most notably, having a pale shell.

**KUWHARU, TAKAREPE, TAKAREPO**
# PINK SUNSET SHELL
*Gari lineolata*

**Distribution:** Three main islands (far northern and southern Te Waipounamu South Island). Lives at 7–31m deep, in soft sediment.

**Size:** Shell length to 68mm.

The delicate pink sunset shell is commonly found on sandy coasts around Aotearoa New Zealand. Their shells have a red, purple or pink interior, and concentric red, orange and cream colour bands on their exterior surface.

**KUWHARU, TAKAREPE, TAKAREPO**
# RAYED SUNSET SHELL
*Gari convexa*

**Distribution:** Three main islands (northern and south-western Te Ika-a-Māui North Island, far northern and southern Te Waipounamu South Island); Rēkohu Wharekauri Chatham Islands. Lives at 6–12m deep, in soft sediment.

**Size:** Shell length to 85mm.

This species is easily mistaken for the pink sunset shell, from which it differs in having radial colour bands in addition to the concentric ones, and, generally, a larger and more inflated shell. Most specimens are orange overall, but purple or white specimens are known.

**KUHARA, KUHARU, KUWHARU, TAKAREPE, TAKAREPO, URUROA, WAHAWAHA**
# STOUT SUNSET SHELL
*Gari stangeri*

**Distribution:** Three main islands; Rēkohu Wharekauri Chatham Islands. Lives at low-tide level to 84m deep, in soft sediment.

**Size:** Shell length to 76mm.

The stout sunset shell, as its name suggests, has a much thicker and stronger shell than the other sunset shell species in Aotearoa. They vary significantly in adult size, colour and pattern. Most often they are pale with some purple radial bands, but some can be orange or grey and resemble a small pipi. Their shells are more rounded than other sunset shell species.

## BASKET SHELL, PEANUT SHELL
*Corbula zelandica*

**Distribution:** Three main islands; Rēkohu Wharekauri Chatham Islands. Lives intertidally to 256m deep, usually in soft substrate habitats with epifaunal communities.

**Size:** Shell length to 15mm.

The basket shell is distinctive in having irregular valves that overlap considerably – resembling an ingrown toenail. They range from cream to yellow, white, grey, purple or pinkish in colour.

### PĀTIOTIO, TETERE MOANA
## ANGEL WING, ROCK BORER
*Barnea similis*

**Distribution:** Three main islands (far northern and eastern Te Waipounamu South Island); Rēkohu Wharekauri Chatham Islands. Lives intertidally and in immediate sublittoral, embedded in soft rock.

**Size:** Shell length to 102mm.

This species burrows into soft rocks such as mudstone. While bivalves are often thought of as having two shells, the rock borer has a third median dorsal shell. They burrow by movement of the valves using the file-like sculpture, possibly aided by a chemical secretion. They are frequently parasitised by the tiny bivalve species *Arthritica crassiformis*.

### KŌMORE, PIPI-KŌMORE, PIPI-TAIARI
## TUSK SHELL
*Antalis nana*

**Distribution:** Both main islands (northern Te Waipounamu South Island). Lives at 15–512m deep, in soft sediment.

**Size:** Shell length to 44mm.

The tusk shell, as its name suggests, resembles the tusk of an elephant. Tusk shells are filter-feeders and live buried in soft sediments with the narrow (respiratory) end projecting from the sediment surface. Māori sometimes used larger, long-extinct tusk shell species to make necklaces. Tusk shells often have strong ribs on the sides of their shells. In deep water there are several tusk shell species, but only *Antalis nana* regularly washes up on beaches.

**KARARURI, PĀUA**
## BLACK-FOOT PĀUA
*Haliotis iris*

**Distribution:** Three main islands; Rēkohu Wharekauri Chatham Islands, Tini Heke Snares Islands. Lives intertidally to at least 14m deep, on rocks.

**Size:** Shell length to 202mm.

This is the largest of three abalone species in Aotearoa New Zealand. Prized as a delicacy, pāua is a popular fishery and aquaculture species. Pāua do not produce anticoagulant, so care should be taken when measuring or handling pāua that might be too small to take. The inside surface of their shells is among the most brightly coloured of all abalone species. The shells are prized as souvenirs in gift-shops; traditionally, they are used by Māori in carvings and earlier in trolling fishing lures.

**HIHIWA, KOROHIWA, PĀUA**
## SILVER PĀUA, YELLOW-FOOT PĀUA
*Haliotis australis*

**Distribution:** Three main islands; Rēkohu Wharekauri Chatham Islands, Tini Heke Snares Islands. Lives intertidally to 12m deep, on rocks.

**Size:** Shell length to 123mm.

The silver pāua is distinctive, with an outer shell that is pale pink, grey, greenish or yellowish, with silver or pink nacre on the inside. The animal has a yellow body, hence the name yellow-foot pāua – the muscle forming most of the body of a gastropod is called the foot.

**KOIO, MARAPEKA**
## VIRGIN PĀUA
*Haliotis virginea*

**Distribution:** Three main islands; Rēkohu Wharekauri Chatham Islands, subantarctic islands. Lives at low-tide level to about 15m deep, on rocks.

**Size:** Shell length to 75mm.

This is the smallest and most diverse of the three pāua species in Aotearoa. Shells in northern Te Ika-a-Māui North Island are often brightly coloured and patterned, ranging from reds to oranges, greys, purples and greens, often overlain with dark and/or pale lines or shapes. Virgin pāua are easily mistaken for juvenile black-foot pāua but have a wider keel around the shell and a dark animal.

## SLIT LIMPET

*Emarginula striatula*

**Distribution:** Three main islands; Rēkohu Wharekauri Chatham Islands, subantarctic islands except Motu Mahue Antipodes Islands. Lives intertidally to 201m deep, on hard substrates.

**Size:** Shell length to 32mm.

This limpet has a distinctive slit running about a quarter of the length of the shell, which is used to improve water flow across the animal's gills. Slit limpet shells range from white to green in colour and have fine network sculpture.

## ELEGANT LIMPET

*Tugali elegans*

**Distribution:** Three main islands; Rēkohu Wharekauri Chatham Islands. Lives intertidally to 256m deep, on hard substrates.

**Size:** Shell length to 55mm.

The elegant limpet is often found under rocks at low-tide level. It has a large golden body that partially engulfs the shell when living. This limpet can be distinguished from a very similar species, *Tugali suteri*, in that the primary cord that runs from the apex to the furthest margin from the apex splits into three rather than two cords as it nears the margin.

### RORI
## DUCK'S BILL SHELL, SHIELD SHELL

*Scutus breviculus*

**Distribution:** Three main islands. Lives intertidally and in immediate sublittoral, on rocks.

**Size:** Shell length to 103mm.

The shield shell has a large black animal that mostly engulfs the yellow- or cream-coloured shell. Because the animal cannot fully retract under the shell when disturbed, it is sometimes termed a semi-slug or sea-slug. They are commonly found in crevices and rockpools and under rocks.

**TIHIPU**
## GREEN TOP SHELL
*Coelotrochus viridis*

**Distribution:** Three main islands; Rēkohu Wharekauri Chatham Islands. Lives intertidally to 64m deep, on rocks and algae.

**Size:** Shell height to 31mm.

The green top shell varies in colour from cream to olive-green, grey and brown. Their shells are often encrusted with other marine species, such as coralline algae (the pink paint-like coating commonly found on coastal rocks), which can make them difficult to spot against the rocks and algae they live on.

**MIMITI, MITIMITI**
## STEPPED TOP SHELL, TIARA TOP SHELL
*Coelotrochus tiaratus*

**Distribution:** Three main islands. Lives from low-tide level to 40m deep, in soft sediments.

**Size:** Shell diameter to 21mm.

The shell of this species is commonly found on beaches, but beach-cast specimens are usually quite worn. The shell is lined with rows of fine nodules and is usually grey in colour. The stepped top shell has a finer sculpture than the similar green top shell, as well as an open umbilicus.

**MATANGONGORE**
## OPAL TOP SHELL
*Cantharidus opalus*

**Distribution:** Three main islands; Rēkohu Wharekauri Chatham Islands, Tini Heke Snares Islands. Lives at low-tide level to 27m deep, on brown algae.

**Size:** Shell height to 53mm.

The name opal top shell stems from the iridescent blues and greens of the nacre inside the aperture, which resembles opals. Juvenile shells, along with mature individuals from northern Te Ika-a-Māui North Island, are usually brightly coloured and strongly patterned. This mollusc was the first species endemic to Aotearoa New Zealand to figure in a scientific publication, in 1774.

### MĀIHI, PŪPŪ, PŪPŪ-MAI
## SPOTTED TOP SHELL
*Diloma aethiops*

**Distribution:** Three main islands; Rēkohu Wharekauri Chatham Islands. Lives intertidally, on rocks.

**Size:** Shell diameter to 38mm.

The spotted top shell is one of the most commonly encountered intertidal snails. Their shells have very fine sculpture and are usually grey, but can appear almost black or have a slightly pink or yellow tinge in some populations.

### WHĒTIKO
## MUDFLAT TOP SHELL
*Diloma subrostratum*

**Distribution:** Three main islands. Lives intertidally, on mud and muddy sand.

**Size:** Shell diameter to 30mm.

The shell of this species ranges in colour from dark grey and light grey to cream or yellow, and often has zebra-like stripes. It is the only *Diloma* species to live on soft substrates rather than rocks or other shells. They live in estuaries and sheltered harbours. Those from Ata Whenua Fiordland are especially strongly patterned.

### MĀIHI
## KNOBBED TOP SHELL
*Diloma bicanaliculatum*

**Distribution:** Three main islands; Rēkohu Wharekauri Chatham Islands. Lives intertidally, on rocks.

**Size:** Shell diameter to 18mm.

The knobbed top shell is the most strongly sculptured of the *Diloma* species. It has rows of flattened keels. The shell is a dark grey with rows of even pale yellow or pinkish spots along the ridges.

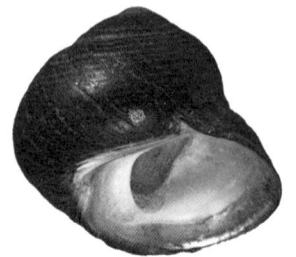

## BLACK TOP SHELL

*Diloma nigerrimum*

**Distribution:** Three main islands; Rēkohu Wharekauri Chatham Islands, Tini Heke Snares Islands, Motu Maha Auckland Islands; also Chile. Lives intertidally, on decaying kelp or rocks.

**Size:** Shell diameter to 30mm.

The black top shell is primarily associated with decaying beach-cast bull kelp. They can occur in their thousands on a single kelp frond, usually at the mid-tide level on very exposed rocky or gravelly beaches. They readily dislodge from the kelp when disturbed (such as by a person walking past), sometimes in their hundreds, making 'clinking' noises as they fall into crevices in the gravel that can sound like hail or heavy rain.

## DARK TOP SHELL

*Diloma zelandicum*

**Distribution:** Three main islands. Lives intertidally, on rocks.

**Size:** Shell diameter to 32mm.

This shell can be difficult to distinguish from the black and arid top shells, but it may usually be distinguished by the uniform black shell and green apertural rim. Their aperture is usually thicker than that of the black top shell.

### MĀIHI
## ARID TOP SHELL

*Diloma aridum*

**Distribution:** Three main islands; Rēkohu Wharekauri Chatham Islands, Motu Maha Auckland Islands. Lives intertidally, on rocks.

**Size:** Shell diameter to 19mm.

The shell of this species is black but commonly has scattered yellowish spots. It has an angular keel and conical overall appearance similar to *Diloma coracina*, *D. bicanaliculatum* or the seldom encountered species *D. durvillaea*.

## SMALL OPAL TOP SHELL

*Micrelenchus dilatatus*

**Distribution:** Three main islands (north-eastern and south-western Te Ika-a-Māui North Island); Rēkohu Wharekauri Chatham Islands. Lives intertidally to about 5m deep, on brown algae.

**Size:** Shell height to 11mm.

The small opal top shell is usually a reddish-brown but can be orange or dark grey and patterned with pale streaks or speckles. The shell is smoother than that of the similar species *Micrelenchus sanguineus*.

## HUTTON'S TOP SHELL

*Micrelenchus huttonii*

**Distribution:** Three main islands. Lives intertidally, on soft sediments or shell.

**Size:** Shell height to 14mm.

Hutton's top shell closely resembles *Micrelenchus tenebrosus*, from which it differs in usually having a taller shell, finer sculpture, and generally living in a more sheltered habitat, such as harbours, rather than on a coastal setting. However, the two species can be found living together near harbour entrances.

## TESSELLATED TOP SHELL

*Micrelenchus tessellatus*

**Distribution:** Three main islands; Rēkohu Wharekauri Chatham Islands. Lives intertidally and in immediate sublittoral, on rocks.

**Size:** Shell height to 9mm.

This is one of the most variable, brightly coloured, and most strongly patterned of all the top shells, ranging from black to green, red and white in colour. They usually live at low tide around the bases of rocks near where they come into contact with sand.

## PINK OPAL TOP SHELL, PINK TOP SHELL

*Micrelenchus purpureus*

**Distribution:** Both main islands (Te Waipounamu South Island as far south as Ōtepoti Dunedin). Lives intertidally to 49m deep, on brown algae.

**Size:** Shell height to 35mm.

The pink top shell ranges in colour from shades of cream to light green or pink. Their shells have very fine sculpture as well as moderate-sized spiral ribs. A similar-looking species, *Micrelenchus burchorum*, occurs at Manawatāwhi Three Kings Islands.

### KOTA
## WHEEL SHELL

*Zethalia zelandica*

**Distribution:** Three main islands (northern and south-western Te Ika-a-Māui North Island). Lives at low-tide level to 6m deep, in sand.

**Size:** Shell diameter to 30mm.

Wheel shells live in the surf zone on sandy beaches. They are capable of moving with surprising speed by using a long muscular foot, which enables them to re-bury themselves when exposed by large waves. They are usually an orange colour with pink tiger-like stripes, although they can be plain orange, with hints of pink and green iridescence showing through the outer shell layers.

## TOOTHED TOP SHELL

*Herpetopoma bellum*

**Distribution:** Both main islands (northern Te Waipounamu South Island as far south as Kaikōura); Rēkohu Wharckauri Chatham Islands. Lives intertidally to 13m deep, under rocks.

**Size:** Shell height to 7mm.

The toothed top shell is often covered with orange sponge, which adheres to the coarsely sculptured shell. The common name reflects the large denticles (bumps) inside the aperture. Several rarer similar-looking species occur in Te Ika-a-Māui North Island.

**MATANGONGORE, MAUREA, REHOREHO**

# TIGER SHELL

*Maurea tigris*

**Distribution:** Three main islands; Rēkohu Wharekauri Chatham Islands. Lives at low-tide level to 206m deep, on rocky reefs and sponge beds.

**Size:** Shell height to 104mm.

The tiger shell is one of the most sought-after shell species in Aotearoa New Zealand. While not actually rare, good specimens are hard to come by and they do not often wash up on beaches. Divers encounter them frequently, often in association with sponges. The shells have vivid orange, cream and red tiger-like stripes, hence their common and Latin names.

# SELECT TIGER SHELL

*Maurea selecta*

**Distribution:** Three main islands; Rēkohu Wharekauri Chatham Islands, Tini Heke Snares Islands. Lives at 27–274m deep, on soft sediment.

**Size:** Shell diameter to 67mm.

This species has a golden-brown dorsal surface with a pale cream underside. They frequently wash up on the Kapiti Coast, but are seldom encountered on beaches in other parts of Aotearoa. A hint of iridescence often shows through the outer layers of the shell.

# SPOTTED TIGER SHELL

*Maurea punctulata*

**Distribution:** Three main islands. Lives at low-tide level to 274m deep, on hard substrates.

**Size:** Shell height to 51mm.

The spotted tiger shell is the most commonly encountered of the tiger shells. A very similar species, Grant's tiger shell (*Maurea granti*), is found throughout most of Aotearoa, and differs subtly in having less rounded whorls near its apex.

## CIRCULAR SAW SHELL
*Astraea heliotropium*

**Distribution:** Three main islands; Rēkohu Wharekauri Chatham Islands. Lives at 10–183m deep, on rocks and among sponges in soft-sediment areas.

**Size:** Shell diameter to 129mm.

This is one of the most distinctive species in Aotearoa New Zealand. Their shells are often covered with encrusting organisms, such as sponges, bryozoans and coralline algae. Their operculum is calcified.

### ATAATA, ATĀTA, KAITANGATA, KŌRAMA, MĀTANGATA, PŪPŪ, PŪPŪ-ATAMANAMA, PŪPŪ-ATAMARAMA, PŪPŪ-KŌRAMA
## CAT'S EYE
*Lunella smaragda*

**Distribution:** Three main islands. Lives intertidally and in immediate sublittoral, on rocks.

**Size:** Shell diameter to 91mm.

The name cat's eye is often applied to the calcified operculum of *Lunella smaragda*. This species lives on rocky shores where they graze on algae. They are an often-overlooked kaimoana species. Large specimens are more common in southern Te Waipounamu South Island and on Rakiura Stewart Island.

### KĀEO, KĀKARA, NGĀEO, NGĀRURA, NGĀRURU, PŪPŪKAREKAWA, PŪPŪ-KAREKAWA, REREKĀKĀ, TOITOI
## COOK'S TURBAN
*Cookia sulcata*

**Distribution:** Three main islands; Rēkohu Wharekauri Chatham Islands. Lives intertidally to 20m deep, on rocks.

**Size:** Shell diameter to 124mm.

This shell is named for Captain James Cook, as it was one of the first mollusc species from Aotearoa to be brought to Europe, in the 1700s. Cook's turbans are usually heavily encrusted with algae and bryozoans. 'Clean' specimens show a sculpture of very fine lamellae atop coarse rows of nodules, which are a reddish brown.

**MATANGĀRAHU, MATAPURA, NGĀRAHU-TATAWA,
NGĀRAHU-TAUA, PEKE**

# BLACK NERITE

*Nerita melanotragus*

**Distribution:** Both main islands (northern Te Waipounamu South Island (rarely) as far south as Kaikōura); Rangitāhua Kermadec Islands; also eastern and southeastern Australia, and Lord Howe and Norfolk Islands. Lives at mid- to high-tide level, on rocks.

**Size:** Shell width to 34mm.

This species resembles several other nerite species found in other parts of the Pacific. Nerites often co-occur with *Diloma* top shells in Aotearoa New Zealand, but they are easily distinguished by a calcified half-moon-shaped operculum and an angular columella.

**NGAETI**

# BLUE PERIWINKLE

*Austrolittorina antipodum*

**Distribution:** Three main islands; Rēkohu Wharekauri Chatham Islands, Rangitāhua Kermadec Islands, Tini Heke Snares Islands. Lives near high-tide level, on rocks.

**Size:** Shell height to 18mm.

The blue periwinkle is one of Aotearoa New Zealand's most abundant mollusc species. They can grow up to 18mm high, however they seldom reach half that height. The shell has a series of blue and white bands, although juvenile and worn shells can appear dark grey or brown.

**NGAETI**

# BROWN PERIWINKLE

*Austrolittorina cincta*

**Distribution:** Three main islands; Rēkohu Wharekauri Chatham Islands, Tini Heke Snares Islands, Motu Maha Auckland Islands. Lives near high-tide level.

**Size:** Shell height to 24mm.

The brown periwinkle grows much larger than the blue periwinkle. As a cold-adapted species, it is less common in northern parts of Te Ika-a-Māui North Island.

### KĀKIHI, RŪHARU
## ENCRUSTED LIMPET
*Patelloida corticata*

**Distribution:** Three main islands. Lives intertidally and in immediate sublittoral.

**Size:** Shell length to 32mm.

This shell is almost always encrusted with coralline algae, which can make it very difficult to see. Cleaned specimens are cream in colour, and the underside of the shell is mostly white but with areas of black and brown near the apex. With their large radial ribs, encrusted limpets can resemble siphon limpets, from which they can easily be distinguished by their pale colour.

### TŪPERE
## FRAGILE LIMPET, FINGERPRINT LIMPET, LINED LIMPET
*Atalacmea fragilis*

**Distribution:** Three main islands. Lives intertidally, under smooth rocks.

**Size:** Shell length to 18mm.

The lined limpet has an extremely fragile shell, coloured green with irregular brown bands that resemble the patterns of a fingerprint. When exposed to sunlight, the animals can move quite quickly to the shaded side of a rock. A second, rarer species occurs in southern Te Waipounamu South Island and on Rakiura Stewart Island; this differs in having a pale rather than green shell, and more densely packed brown colour bands.

### KĀKIHI, NGAKIHI
## ORNATE LIMPET
*Cellana ornata*

**Distribution:** Three main islands. Lives intertidally, on rocks.

**Size:** Shell length to 54mm.

The ornate limpet lives on mid- to high-tide rocks on exposed shores. Their shells range from brown to grey, and radial rows of pale spots are usually present – distinguishing ornate limpets from other *Cellana* species.

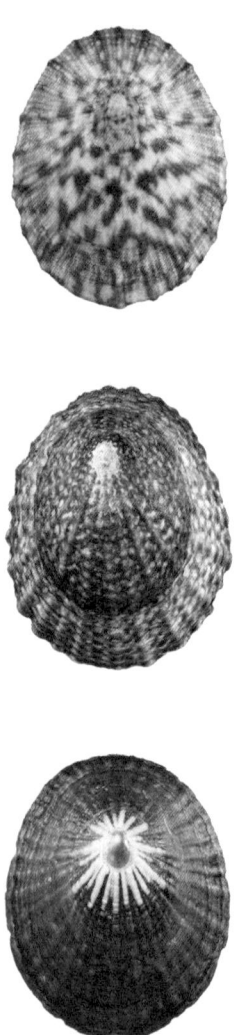

**KĀKIHI, NGAKIHI**
# TORTOISESHELL LIMPET
*Cellana radians*

**Distribution:** Three main islands. Lives intertidally, on rocks.

**Size:** Shell length to 68mm.

This is one of the most variable limpet species in Aotearoa New Zealand. Their shells can be white, grey, brown or almost black, and variably and brightly patterned. In Te Ika-a-Māui North Island populations, a common marbled pattern resembles that of a tortoise's shell, hence the common name.

# DENTICULATE LIMPET
*Cellana denticulata*

**Distribution:** Both main islands (Te Rerenga Wairua Cape Reinga and Cape Maria van Diemen, eastern and southern Te Ika-a-Māui North Island, and north-eastern Te Waipounamu South Island as far south as Taumanu-o-te-Waka-a-Māui Kaikōura Peninsula). Lives intertidally, on rocks.

**Size:** Shell length to 84mm.

This limpet has a very strange distribution. From northern Te Ika-a-Māui North Island to Māhia Peninsula this species is rare and mostly restricted to offshore islands or headlands. It seems possible that these populations are relicts of a greater distribution and abundance in northern Te Ika-a-Māui and Manawatāwhi Three Kings Islands during the last ice age. The denticulate limpet can easily be distinguished from the superficially similar species *Cellana strigilis* by the regular denticles (bumps) along the radial ridges of the shell.

# STAR LIMPET
*Cellana stellifera*

**Distribution:** Both main islands. Lives at low tide and in immediate sublittoral, on rocks.

**Size:** Shell length to 64mm.

The star limpet usually lives lower on the shoreline than the other *Cellana* species with which it co-occurs. Their shells are usually a dark reddish brown, which fades to orange after death. In combination with the radial ribs, the pale area normally found near the apex resembles a star.

**KUKUKUROAROA, PAPATAI**
# COMMON TOWER SHELL
*Maoricolpus roseus*

**Distribution:** Three main islands; Rēkohu Wharekauri Chatham Islands, Rangitāhua Kermadec Islands, Tini Heke Snares Islands; also introduced to southern and eastern Australia. Lives at low-tide level to at least 102m deep, on soft sediments.

**Size:** Shell height to 85mm.

The tower shell is a common and widespread species. Pure white specimens are fairly common on the continental shelf off the coast of Otago. This is not an example of true albinism, as the animals and opercula still have pigment. Those from the nearby Otago Harbour, and other regions, are either light or dark brown.

# SMALL TOWER SHELL
*Stiracolpus pagoda*

**Distribution:** Te Ika-a-Māui North Island (north-eastern as far south-east as Whangaparāoa Cape Runaway and Te Mānuka-o-Hotunui Manukau Harbour). Lives at 4–59m deep, on soft sediments.

**Size:** Shell height to 37mm.

This is one of a group of several similar tower shell species that occur around Aotearoa New Zealand. Their shells are usually dark brown, but they can be cream or light brown in colour. They are often intricately patterned with wavy stripes.

# LINED TOWER SHELL
*Zeacolpus vittatus*

**Distribution:** Both main islands (far northern and south-western Te Waipounamu South Island). Lives at 18–183m deep, on soft sediment.

**Size:** Shell height to 98mm.

This shell is similar in size to the common tower shell, from which it differs in being relatively more elongate and in having numerous even brown lines running the length of the cream-coloured shell.

## SMOOTH SLIPPER SHELL

*Maoricrypta sodalis*

**Distribution:** Three main islands; Tini Heke Snares Islands. Lives intertidally to 925m deep, on hard substrates.

**Size:** Shell length to 43mm.

This mollusc usually lives inside the whorls of dead gastropods. Their shells can be irregular shapes depending on the surface on which they were living. The name slipper shell refers to a little flap of shell on the ventral side that gives them a resemblance to some casual footwear.

### NGĀKIHI
## CONVEX SLIPPER SHELL

*Maoricrypta monoxyla*

**Distribution:** Te Ika-a-Māui North Island (as far south-east as Whangaparāoa Cape Runaway). Lives intertidally to 15m deep, on hard substrates.

**Size:** Shell length to 27mm.

The convex slipper shell usually lives on the outside of other shells or small rocks, resulting in a convex shape. They can closely resemble the smooth slipper shell.

### NGĀKIHI
## RIBBED SLIPPER SHELL

*Maoricrypta costata*

**Distribution:** Te Ika-a-Māui North Island (as far south as Māhia Peninsula). Lives intertidally to 47m deep, on rocks and shells.

**Size:** Shell length to 55mm.

The ribbed slipper shell is quite variable in terms of shape, sculpture and colour. They usually have prominent ribs running from the apex to the furthest margin, and come in cream, gold or brown colours. A similar species, *Maoricrypta youngi*, differs in not growing as large and having a smoother shell.

**NGĀKIHI KOPIA**
## HAIRY SLIPPER SHELL
*Sigapatella novaezelandiae*

**Distribution:** Three main islands; Rēkohu Wharekauri Chatham Islands, subantarctic islands except Motu Mahue Antipodes Islands. Lives intertidally to 220m deep, on rocks and shells.

**Size:** Shell diameter to 42mm.

This species is roughly circular with a thick brown periostracum, which is covered with coarse hairs. The carbonate part of the shell is mostly white but usually has purple or brown areas.

## SMALL SLIPPER SHELL
*Sigapatella tenuis*

**Distribution:** Three main islands; Rēkohu Wharekauri Chatham Islands. Lives at 2–315m deep, on shells.

**Size:** Shell diameter to 24mm.

The small slipper shell is a conical species that can range in colour from whites to browns or purples. The shell does not grow as large or as thick as the hairy slipper shell.

## NEW ZEALAND WORM SHELL
*Thylacodes zelandicus*

**Distribution:** North-eastern Te Ika-a-Māui North Island, northern and south-western Te Waipounamu South Island. Lives intertidally to 25m deep, on hard substrates.

**Size:** Shell length to at least 65mm.

This is one of several mollusc species that closely resemble tube-worms (annelids). The New Zealand worm shell has a sculpture of several rows of beads or ribs running along the shell, and is usually golden or brown in colour. Other worm shell species can be smooth and occur in large clusters under rocks.

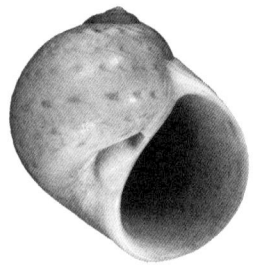

### KOETI
# MUDFLAT HORN SHELL
*Zeacumantus lutulentus*

**Distribution:** Northern and south-western Te Ika-a-Māui North Island, northern and south-western Te Waipounamu South Island. Lives intertidally, on mudflats.

**Size:** Shell length to 34mm.

A common yet often overlooked species, whose shells are often quite eroded, even in life. Uneroded specimens have numerous axial ribs, and while mostly grey or brown, can have hints of blue, white and yellow on their shells.

### KOETI
# BLACK HORN SHELL
*Zeacumantus subcarinatus*

**Distribution:** Te Ika-a-Māui North Island (north-western Mohua Golden Bay) and eastern Te Waipounamu South Island; Rēkohu Wharekauri Chatham Islands; also introduced to New South Wales, Australia, and now established there. Lives intertidally, in rockpools.

**Size:** Shell height to 19mm.

This shell is smaller and has finer sculpture than the mudflat horn shell. The black horn shell normally lives in association with rocks and can be found in mid-tide rockpools or under rock slabs.

# NECKLACE SHELL, NEW ZEALAND MOON SNAIL
*Tanea zelandica*

**Distribution:** Three main islands; Rēkohu Wharekauri Chatham Islands, Tini Heke Snares Islands, Motu Maha Auckland Islands, Moutere Hauriri Bounty Islands. Lives at 0–128m deep, in sand.

**Size:** Shell height to 35mm.

These shells are normally a golden colour with rows of reddish-brown beads. However, off Otago pure white shells are sometimes found. The necklace shell feeds on other shellfish by drilling a hole through their shells. They live in sand, emerge at night to feed, and have a calcified operculum that completely seals their aperture when disturbed.

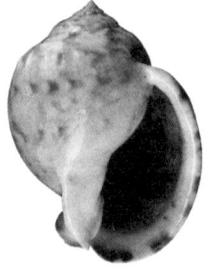

**KAIKAI-KARORO, TAKAI, TOTORERE**

# LARGE OSTRICH FOOT

*Struthiolaria papulosa*

**Distribution:** Three main islands. Lives at low-tide level to 39m deep, in soft sediments.

**Size:** Shell height to 106mm.

This species gets its name from its small, spiked operculum and long peach-coloured foot, which vaguely resembles the foot of an ostrich. They use their feet to bury themselves in the sediment to escape predators.

**TAKAI, TĀKAI**

# SMALL OSTRICH FOOT

*Pelicaria vermis*

**Distribution:** Both main islands. Lives at low-tide level to 82m deep, in soft sediments.

**Size:** Shell height to 59mm.

This species resembles the large ostrich foot but has a more rounded aperture and does not grow as large. Their shells range from reddish to yellowish brown and can have pale wavy lines.

# HELMET SHELL

*Semicassis pyrum*

**Distribution:** Three main islands; Rēkohu Wharekauri Chatham Islands and Chatham Rise, Tini Heke Snares Islands; also southern Australia. Lives from shallow sublittoral to 478m deep, in soft sediments.

**Size:** Shell height to 110mm.

Shells from deeper water tend to be pale and less patterned. A similar, less common species, *Semicassis labiata*, occurs with the common helmet shell around much of Te Ika-a-Māui North Island, but differs in usually having a pink and purple apex as well as rows of pale spots along the shell.

## CASK SHELL, TUN SHELL
*Tonna tankervillii*

**Distribution:** Te Ika-a-Māui North Island as far south as Whanganui, and Patea Doubtful Sound; also eastern Australia. Lives at low-tide level to 55m deep, in sand.

**Size:** Shell height to 252mm.

The cask shell is very popular with shell collectors and beachcombers because of its large size and colourful and strongly patterned shells. They can wash ashore in large numbers following a storm. During calmer times, collectors often have to make do with tantalising fragments.

### AWANUI, PŪPŪ-TARA, PŪPŪ-TATARA, PŪTARA, PŪTARATARA, PŪTĀTARA, TĀTARA, TŪTEURE
## LARGE TRUMPET
*Charonia lampas*

**Distribution:** Three main islands; Rēkohu Wharekauri Chatham Islands, Rangitāhua Kermadec Islands; distributed worldwide in temperate seas. Lives intertidally to 205m deep, in a range of habitats.

**Size:** Shell height to 310mm.

In Aotearoa New Zealand this species is most commonly found in shallow water off northern Te Ika-a-Māui North Island. It is prized by Māori as the basis for pūtātara (trumpets). In recently made pūtātara, the larger and consistently brightly coloured tropical triton trumpet (*Charonia tritonis*; not found on mainland Aotearoa) is often used instead. The large trumpet can be shades of vivid red, purple, buff or brown, and is often strongly patterned.

## AUSTRALASIAN TRITON
*Ranella australasia*

**Distribution:** Both main islands; Rēkohu Wharekauri Chatham Islands, Rangitāhua Kermadec Islands; also Australia, Lord Howe Island and Norfolk Island. Lives at low-tide level to 145m deep, in a range of habitats.

**Size:** Shell height to 123mm.

This mollusc has a dark reddish-brown or pale orange-brown shell and a thin grey-brown periostracum covered in numerous fine, short hairs.

## SWOLLEN TRITON

*Argobuccinum pustulosum*

**Distribution:** Both main islands; Rēkohu Wharekauri Chatham Islands, Rangitāhua Kermadec Islands, Tini Heke Snares Islands; also southern Africa, South Atlantic and southern Australia. Lives intertidally to 128m deep, in a range of habitats.

**Size:** Shell height to 136mm.

The swollen triton is a large and rounded species that has a thin grey-brown periostracum covered in fine, short hairs and a pale shell covered with fine reddish and brown lines.

## SPENGLER'S TRUMPET

*Cabestana spengleri*

**Distribution:** Both main islands; Rēkohu Wharekauri Chatham Islands, Rangitāhua Kermadec Islands; also eastern and south-eastern Australia. Lives intertidally to 40m deep, on rocks.

**Size:** Shell height to 188mm.

Spengler's trumpet shells comprise a thick, translucent, light brown periostracum and a golden or cream-coloured calcified shell. A much rarer superficially similar species, *Cabestana tabulata*, generally differs in having finer sculpture.

## HAIRY TRITON

*Monoplex parthenopeus*

**Distribution:** Both main islands (northern and south-western Te Waipounamu South Island); Rēkohu Wharekauri Chatham Islands, Rangitāhua Kermadec Islands; also Indo-West Pacific, Atlantic and Mediterranean, Lord Howe Island and Norfolk Island. Lives intertidally to 100m deep, in a range of habitats.

**Size:** Shell height to 142mm.

This species has a thick, dark brown or golden periostracum lined with dozens of long hairs. Underneath, the calcified part of the shell is buff, orange or brown in colour. The animals are brightly coloured and patterned.

## LARGE VIOLET SNAIL

*Janthina janthina*

**Distribution:** Three main islands; Rēkohu Wharekauri Chatham Islands, Rangitāhua Kermadec Islands; distributed worldwide in tropical and temperate seas. Pelagic.

**Size:** Shell diameter to 50mm.

Like all violet snails, this is a pelagic species that builds a raft out of bubbles and floats on the ocean surface, where it hunts protozoan 'jellyfish' such as the bluebottle (*Physalia* spp.). The purple and white shells are counter-shaded: the white apex faces down, making the snail hard for predators to see from below against the pale sky, while the purple part of the shell renders it difficult for birds to spot from the air.

## SMALL VIOLET SNAIL

*Janthina exigua*

**Distribution:** Three main islands (northern Te Waipounamu South Island); Rēkohu Wharekauri Chatham Islands, Rangitāhua Kermadec Islands; distributed worldwide in tropical and temperate seas. Pelagic.

**Size:** Shell height to 23mm.

This snail seldom exceeds 10mm in length. Their shells are easily distinguished from the large violet snail, or the less common globose violet snail (*Janthina globosa*), by the presence of numerous fine chevron-shaped varices (ribs) and their relatively small size. The rarer *Janthina umbilicata* is harder to distinguish but has finer sculpture and is usually a different shade of purple.

## WENTLETRAP

*Cirsotrema zelebori*

**Distribution:** Three main islands; Rēkohu Wharekauri Chatham Islands, Rangitāhua Kermadec Islands, Motu Maha Auckland Islands, Motu Mahue Antipodes Islands; also southern Norfolk Ridge. Lives at 8–206m deep, in sand.

**Size:** Shell height to 29mm.

Very popular with shell collectors, the elegant elongate white shells of this species have numerous distinctive varices (ribs) running the length of the shell. Like other members of the wentletrap family, it probably eats sea anemones. The wentletrap lives all around Aotearoa New Zealand, but is seldom encountered except in northern Te Ika-a-Māui North Island, where several smaller species are also found.

## TARON
*Taron dubius*

**Distribution:** Te Ika-a-Māui North Island as far south as Māhia Peninsula, and Whakatū Nelson (presumably introduced there by shipping). Lives intertidally to 23m deep, on rocks.

**Size:** Shell height to 22mm.

This species has dark brown shells with white or pale orange apertures and siphonal canals. The shells are often heavily encrusted with coralline algae. The animals are bright red in colour, in striking contrast to their dull shells.

### HUAMUTU
## LINED WHELK
*Buccinulum linea*

**Distribution:** Three main islands (northern Te Waipounamu South Island as far south as Ōtautahi Christchurch); Rēkohu Wharekauri Chatham Islands. Lives intertidally to 82m deep, on hard substrates.

**Size:** Shell height to 42mm.

Shells are usually pale with consistent reddish-brown lines, but can be shades of brown, orange, purple or red, and either lined, without a colour pattern, or covered with irregular blotches of colour. These carnivores live in association with rocks or hard substrates such as shell, bryozoan or sponge beds.

## NORTHERN LINED WHELK
*Buccinulum vittatum*

**Distribution:** Te Ika-a-Māui North Island as far south-east as Whangaparāoa Cape Runaway. Lives intertidally to 18m deep, on rocks and shells.

**Size:** Shell height to 28mm.

The northern lined whelk is one of the most variable gastropod species in the country. Their shells can be pale, black, brown or orange and their pattern can be fine lines, large blotches or absent entirely; even the shell shape is highly variable. Similar species occur in southern Te Ika-a-Māui North Island and in Te Waipounamu South Island, Rakiura Stewart Island and Rēkohu Wharekauri Chatham Islands.

## KĀKARA
# KNOBBED WHELK

*Austrofusus glans*

**Distribution:** Three main islands; Rēkohu Wharekauri Chatham Islands and western Chatham Rise. Lives at low-tide level to 1420m deep, in soft substrates.

**Size:** Shell height to 88mm.

This whelk lives in sand and mud environments. Their shells are usually pale and often have purple-red bands, blotches or lines. Many fossil knobbed whelk species are found in mudstones around Aotearoa New Zealand.

## KAWARI
# SPECKLED WHELK

*Cominella adspersa*

**Distribution:** Both main islands (northern Te Waipounamu South Island as far south as Kaikōura); Rēkohu Wharekauri Chatham Islands. Lives intertidally to 48m deep, in a range of habitats.

**Size:** Shell height to 74mm.

The speckled whelk predominantly lives in sand and mud habitats but can sometimes be found among rocks. They have a heavy shell to protect them from predators.

# SPOTTED WHELK

*Cominella maculosa*

**Distribution:** Both main islands (northern Te Waipounamu South Island as far south as Ōtautahi Christchurch); Rēkohu Wharekauri Chatham Islands. Lives intertidally to 2m deep, on rocks and in sand among rocky reefs.

**Size:** Shell height to 58mm.

This whelk is very similar to the speckled whelk, from which it differs in being more elongate and having larger pale spots, rather than small dark spots (speckles). Spotted whelks lay large communal clusters of pale elongate egg masses under rocks.

**KAWARI**
# MUDFLAT WHELK
*Cominella glandiformis*

**Distribution:** Three main islands; Rēkohu Wharekauri Chatham Islands. Lives intertidally, on mud and muddy sand.

**Size:** Shell height to 44mm.

As its common name suggests, the mudflat whelk lives in muddy areas in harbours and estuaries. Being scavengers, they accumulate in large numbers when a dead animal is detected. They range in colour from black to orange or cream, and often have some blue on their shells.

**KAWARI**
# ORANGE-MOUTHED WHELK
*Cominella virgata*

**Distribution:** Northern and south-western Te Ika-a-Māui North Island and northern Te Waipounamu South Island. Lives intertidally to 6m deep, on rocks.

**Size:** Shell height to 43mm.

The orange-mouthed whelk lives on rocky reefs. Specimens from northern Te Ika-a-Māui North Island usually have more dark-colour bands on the shell. Female whelks deposit little clam-shell-shaped egg masses, each of which contains several young.

# QUOY'S WHELK
*Cominella quoyana*

**Distribution:** Te Ika-a-Māui North Island as far south as Māhia Peninsula. Lives from low tide to 51m deep, in soft sediments, often in association with bivalve beds or rocky reefs.

**Size:** Shell height to 26mm.

Quoy's whelk is an extremely variable species in terms of coloration and pattern. The shells are usually cream but can be pink, purple, chestnut brown, green or almost black. They emerge at night to feed.

**KAIKAI TIO**
## ROUGH OYSTER BORER
*Haustrum scobina*

**Distribution:** Both main islands (far northern Te Waipounamu South Island); Rēkohu Wharekauri Chatham Islands. Lives intertidally, on rocks.

**Size:** Shell height to 41mm.

Despite their name, rough oyster borers mostly feed on barnacles rather than oysters, into which they drill using their tough radulae (a tooth-covered feeding structure). Their shells are usually grey with a mixture of dark and pale areas and knobbly sculpture.

## OYSTER BORER
*Haustrum albomarginatum*

**Distribution:** Three main islands (north-eastern and western Te Ika-a-Māui North Island); Rēkohu Wharekauri Chatham Islands. Lives intertidally, on rocks.

**Size:** Shell height to 30mm.

The oyster borer cannot be reliably distinguished from the rough oyster borer, although it normally differs in having a smoother shell and more distinctive spiral colour bands. Oyster borers most commonly occur on mid-tide rocks, where they feed by drilling into barnacles.

**KĀEO, KĀKARA, NGĀEO**
## DARK ROCK SHELL
*Haustrum haustorium*

**Distribution:** Both main islands; Rēkohu Wharekauri Chatham Islands. Lives intertidally, on rocks.

**Size:** Shell height to 81mm.

The dark rock shell grows much larger than the closely related oyster borer species, and has a more varied diet. The aperture is proportionately larger, too, when compared against similarly sized specimens of the oyster borers.

## LARGE TROPHON

*Zeatrophon ambiguus*

**Distribution:** Three main islands; Rēkohu Wharekauri Chatham Islands. Lives at low tide level to 73m deep, in soft sediments.

**Size:** Shell height to 64mm.

The large trophon is quite variable – their shells are usually white, but can be cream, purple or almost brown in colour. Juveniles and specimens from sheltered carbonate-rich environments can have large wavy frills.

## COMMON TROPHON

*Xymene plebeius*

**Distribution:** Three main islands (northern and eastern Te Waipounamu South Island). Lives intertidally to 3m deep, on hard substrates in areas of soft sediment.

**Size:** Shell height to 23mm.

The common trophon predominantly lives in muddy habitats within harbours, but in association with rocks or other, larger, shells. They feed by drilling circular holes through the shells of other mollusc species.

## TRAVERS' MUREX

*Lamellitrophon traversi*

**Distribution:** Both main islands; Rēkohu Wharekauri Chatham Islands. Lives intertidally to 18m deep, on rocks.

**Size:** Shell height to 25mm.

Travers' murex is part of a group of common but often overlooked murex species that live in shallow water on rocky reefs. They are often covered in coralline algae, which is difficult to remove and makes it difficult to spot the murexes or identify a particular species.

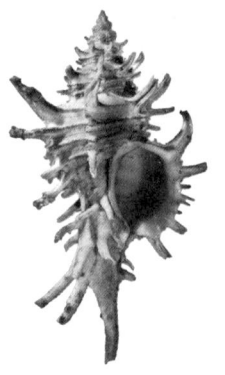

## SPINY MUREX
*Poirieria zelandica*

**Distribution:** Both main islands; Rēkohu Wharekauri Chatham Islands and Challenger Plateau. Lives at low-tide level to 540m deep, in soft sediments.

**Size:** Shell height to 89mm.

One of the most distinctive and sought-after shells in Aotearoa New Zealand, the spiny murex lives in sand and mud, emerging at night to hunt. Their rows of spines serve to protect them against predation by fish. Shell collectors used to sometimes gather spiny murex by towing a frayed rope along the sea floor, or by lowering a stocking with bait inside on a line. The spines would get caught in the rope or stocking, allowing the collector to reel in the murex.

## OCTAGONAL MUREX
*Murexsul octogonus*

**Distribution:** Off Cape Maria van Diemen, and north-eastern and south-western Te Ika-a-Māui North Island. Lives from low-tide level to 100m deep, in a range of habitats.

**Size:** Shell height to 90mm.

The octagonal murex can be pale, brown, black or even purple. They live on rocky reefs, among bivalve beds in sand, or in bryozoan coral banks. The length of their spines varies throughout their distribution, in part due to their habitat.

#### HOPETEA, TAWIRI
## WHITE ROCK SHELL
*Dicathais orbita*

**Distribution:** Both main islands (Te Waipounamu South Island as far south as Haast); Rēkohu Wharekauri Chatham Islands, Rangitāhua Kermadec Islands; also Australia, Lord Howe Island and Norfolk Island. Lives intertidally to 45m deep, on rocks.

**Size:** Shell height to 120mm.

The shell of this species ranges in colour from white to dark brown. Some specimens have extremely pronounced spiral ribs, which may serve to strengthen the shell against predation from crabs or drilling by octopus. White rock shells tend to live on exposed rocky coastlines in crevices and under overhangs, and lay eggs in large communal clusters. The egg capsules in the outer parts of the cluster are often a bright purple and unpalatable, a defence against would-be predators.

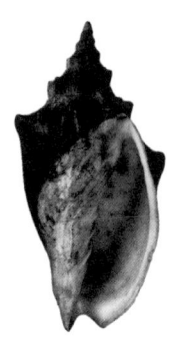

**PUHAURIROA, PŪPŪ RORE, PŪPŪ-RORE,
TĀKUPU, TIKOAKA, UERE**

## ARABIC VOLUTE

*Alcithoe arabica*

**Distribution:** Three main islands. Lives at low-tide level to 146m deep, on soft sediments.

**Size:** Shell height to 236mm.

The Arabic volute is named for the intricate dark-brown patterns on the shell that can resemble written script. These animals emerge from the sediment at night to hunt for prey. They deposit large, bulbous, white egg clusters, each containing multiple young, on hard surfaces such as other shells.

## SMALL VOLUTE

*Alcithoe fusus*

**Distribution:** Three main islands (northern and south-western Te Ika-a-Māui North Island, northern and eastern Te Waipounamu South Island). Lives at 22–370m deep, on soft sediments.

**Size:** Shell height to 85mm.

This species usually differs from the Arabic volute in lacking a flattened plate near the siphonal notch and having only four rather than five to six columellar plaits. The colour pattern of the small volute comprises a series of fine interlocking wavy lines and lacks the larger blotches common in the Arabic volute.

## DWARF OLIVE

*Amalda novaezelandiae*

**Distribution:** Te Ika-a-Māui North Island and northern Te Waipounamu South Island as far south as Akaroa. Lives at 5–198m deep, in soft sediments.

**Size:** Shell height to 15mm.

The dwarf olive is very similar to *Amalda northlandica*, from which it differs in being more elongate and, generally, less brightly coloured.

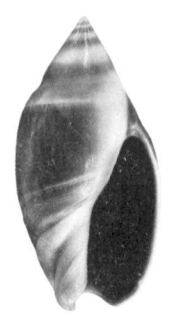

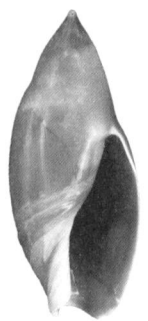

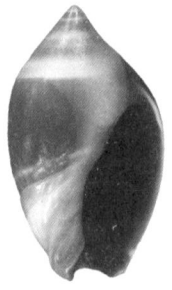

**PŪPŪ PIATĀTA, PŪPŪ-RORE, TE OUARA, TIKOAKA, UERE**

# DARK OLIVE, SOUTHERN OLIVE

*Amalda australis*

**Distribution:** Northern and south-western Te Ika-a-Māui North Island, and northern Te Waipounamu South Island as far south as Ōamaru. Lives at low-tide level to 37m deep, in soft sediments.

**Size:** Shell height to 52mm.

The dark olive can sometimes be found emerging out of the sand at low tide. The animal is pale and fully encompasses the shell when active. The central band on the shell is often a pale blue-grey, when the rest of the shell is dark brown.

**UERE**

# BROWN OLIVE

*Amalda mucronata*

**Distribution:** Three main islands (northern and south-western Te Waipounamu South Island, western Rakiura Stewart Island). Lives at extreme low-tide level (rarely) to 410m deep, in soft sediments.

**Size:** Shell height to 62mm.

This species grows much larger than the dark olive. Shells are normally a light golden-brown colour, with pale bands. Their apex is also usually more rounded (blunt) than the dark olive.

# DEPRESSED OLIVE

*Amalda depressa*

**Distribution:** Northern and south-western Te Ika-a-Māui North Island, and northern Te Waipounamu South Island as far south as Ōtautahi Christchurch. Lives at low-tide level to 27m deep, in soft sediments.

**Size:** Shell height to 20mm.

Closely resembling the dark olive, the depressed olive differs in being far smaller at maturity. Depressed olives are highly variable in size and shape throughout their distribution.

## NEW ZEALAND TOWER SHELL

*Phenatoma zealandicum*

**Distribution:** Te Ika-a-Māui North Island and northern Te Waipounamu South Island as far south as Akaroa. Lives at low-tide level to 35m deep, in soft sediments.

**Size:** Shell height to 34mm.

The New Zealand tower shell is scarcer than the rosy tower shell. Their shells are a pale pinkish or yellowish colour, and are glossier due to having less fine sculpture.

## ROSY TOWER SHELL

*Phenatoma roseum*

**Distribution:** Three main islands; Rēkohu Wharekauri Chatham Islands. Lives at low-tide level to 131m deep, in soft sediments.

**Size:** Shell height to 37mm.

The shell of this species can be pale or vivid pink or purple in colour. In combination with the fine sculpture on the shell, this makes it highly desirable among shell collectors. All tower shells have a distinctive notch at the apical end of their apertures.

## COMMON AUGER

*Duplicaria tristis*

**Distribution:** Three main islands (northern and eastern Te Waipounamu South Island); also southern and eastern Australia. Lives at low-tide level to 11m deep, in soft sediments.

**Size:** Shell height to 24mm.

The common auger is a highly variable species, with shells ranging in colour from dark brown to cream or orange. They spend most of their lives buried in sand and emerge at night to feed.

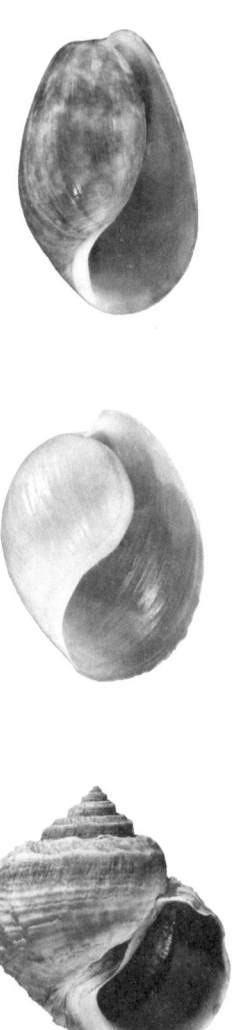

### PŪPŪ WAHAROA, PŪPŪ-WAHAROA
## BROWN BUBBLE SHELL
*Bulla quoyii*

**Distribution:** North-eastern Te Ika-a-Māui North Island as far south as Te Awanui Tauranga Harbour; also Indo-Pacific waters. Lives at low-tide level to 20m deep, in soft sediments.

**Size:** Shell height to 61mm.

This species lives in sheltered areas in northern Te Ika-a-Māui North Island. A similar, rarer species, *Bulla vernicosa*, co-occurs in the same area. It differs in not growing as large, and having a thicker shell and a straighter apertural margin.

### PŪPŪ TUATEA
## FRAGILE BUBBLE SHELL, WHITE BUBBLE SHELL
*Papawera zelandiae*

**Distribution:** Both main islands. Lives intertidally, in muddy habitats.

**Size:** Shell height to 29mm.

The fragile bubble shell inhabits estuaries and muddy harbours around Aotearoa New Zealand. The delicate cream-coloured shell is mostly enclosed in the animal when it is active and emerged from sediment; the animal is dark brown or grey with pale flecks. It is common for them to die off in their thousands over the summer months.

### KARAHŪ, KARAHUE, KAREHU, KORIAKAI, TAKAREPU, TĀTOKO, TITOKO, WĒTIWHA, WHĒTIKO, WHĒTIKOTIKO
## MUDFLAT SNAIL
*Amphibola crenata*

**Distribution:** Three main islands; Rēkohu Wharekauri Chatham Islands. Lives intertidally, on mud.

**Size:** Shell diameter to 39mm.

As its common English name suggests, this snail inhabits muddy estuaries, all around Aotearoa. The shells are often highly eroded, but uneroded specimens can have delicate frills and be a range of yellows, oranges, browns and creams. Mature and eroded specimens tend to be darker greys and browns.

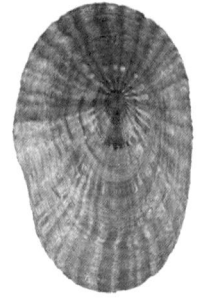

**ANGA NUI NIHO**
# BANDED EAR SHELL
*Pleuroloba costellaris*

**Distribution:** Both main islands (northern Te Waipounamu South Island). Lives near high-tide level, under rocks and among reeds.

**Size:** Shell height to 15mm.

This snail lives in brackish water around estuaries and river mouths, often at or even above the high-tide level, on coastal reeds and grasses or under rocks. Their shells range in colour from black to brown or green, often patterned with horizontal colour bands. Several smaller ear shell species are commonly found under rocks and decaying seaweed at high-tide level.

**KĀKIHI, NGĀKIHI, PIRITOKA**
# LARGE SIPHON LIMPET
*Benhamina obliquata*

**Distribution:** Three main islands; Motu Maha Auckland Islands. Lives intertidally, on rocks.

**Size:** Shell length to 66mm.

The large siphon limpet is seldom encountered living. In summer, their circular yellow egg masses often cover the faces of the exposed rocky shores and cliffs on which they live. Shells often have an orange colour on the inside. This species is an air-breather, being more closely related to land snails than to other marine limpets.

**KĀKIHI AWAAWA, NGĀKIHI AWAAWA**
# SMALL SIPHON LIMPET
*Siphonaria australis*

**Distribution:** Three main islands; Rēkohu Wharekauri Chatham Islands, Tini Heke Snares Islands, Motu Maha Auckland Islands. Lives intertidally, on hard substrates.

**Size:** Shell length to 32mm.

This limpet is commonly found at the mid- and upper-tide marks on rocky shores all around Aotearoa New Zealand. Small siphon limpets are seldom symmetrical. The term 'siphon limpet' refers to a bulge on the side of the shell where their air-breathing organs are. A similar, less common species, *Siphonaria propria*, is easily confused with the small siphon limpet.

## COMMON CHAROPA SNAIL
*Charopa coma*

**Distribution:** Three main islands. Lives under decaying wood and in leaf litter.

**Size:** Shell diameter to 7mm.

This snail is very broadly distributed throughout Aotearoa New Zealand. Its brown and orange bands make it very well camouflaged among the leaf litter and fallen logs where it lives. Aotearoa has hundreds of similar small snail species.

## FLAX SNAIL
*Maoristylus hongii*

**Distribution:** North-eastern Te Ika-a-Māui North Island as far south as Aotea Great Barrier Island (historical). Lives in coastal forests.

**Size:** Shell height to 85mm.

Flax snails are highly vulnerable to predation by pigs, thrushes and rats, and are now confined to a few protected headlands and islands in northern Aotearoa. They are herbivorous, moving very little in their lifetime if near a suitable food plant. A second species, *Maoristylus ambagiosus* or pūpūwhakarongotaua, lives in the northern tip of Te Ika-a-Māui North Island and differs in having a more rounded apertural margin.

### KĀKAHI
## FRESHWATER MUSSEL
*Echyridella menziesii*

**Distribution:** Both main islands. Lives in streams, rivers and lakes.

**Size:** Shell length to 103mm.

Freshwater mussels are highly variable in shape, ranging from almost circular to thin and elongate. The te reo Māori name refers to the bright olive-green of their shells when not covered in algae or precipitate. Their larvae are parasitic on the gills of freshwater fishes, which enables them to disperse upstream within river systems. Freshwater mussels can live for several decades. The rarer species *Echyridella aucklandica* lives in northern Te Ika-a-Māui North Island as well as Lakes Wairarapa and Hauroko, and a third species lives in north-western Te Waipounamu South Island.

**PŪPŪRANGI**
# KAURI SNAIL
*Paryphanta busbyi*

**Distribution:** Northern Te Ika-a-Māui North Island (natural); also translocated populations near Tāmaki Makaurau Auckland, Tauranga and Rotorua. Lives in forests and scrub.

**Size:** Shell diameter to 79mm.

The kauri snail has an olive-green shell with a blue-grey interior and an almost black body. They hide in leaf litter by day and emerge at night to hunt earthworms and other invertebrates; they have been known to cannibalise smaller snails. These snails are especially vulnerable to predation by rats and pigs and are legally protected to help ensure their long-term survival.

# HOCHSTETTER'S SNAIL
*Powelliphanta hochstetteri*

**Distribution:** Northern Te Waipounamu South Island. Lives in mid-altitude forests.

**Size:** Shell diameter to 75mm.

Hochstetter's snail is one of the most brightly coloured and strongly patterned of the giant snails in Aotearoa New Zealand. They hunt earthworms at night and hide in the leaf litter by day. While still common in parts of their distribution, this species, like most giant snails in Aotearoa, is very vulnerable to drought and predation by rats, possums and weka, among others. All giant snails, and their shells, are legally protected.

# WAINUIA
*Wainuia urnula*

**Distribution:** Southern and eastern Te Ika a-Māui North Island. Lives in forests.

**Size:** Shell diameter to 28mm.

When living, these snails appear black. They have a thin, dark brown translucent shell and a dark grey, blue or purple body. They are carnivorous, feeding on amphipods (hoppers), worms and other snails. Other very similar-looking *Wainuia* species occur in northern Te Waipounamu South Island and central Te Ika-a-Māui North Island.

## FRESHWATER SNAIL, NEW ZEALAND MUD SNAIL
*Potamopyrgus antipodarum*

**Distribution:** Three main islands; Rēkohu Wharekauri Chatham Islands; also North and South America, Europe and Asia. Lives in a range of freshwater habitats.

**Size:** Shell height to 12mm.

This is probably the most abundant non-marine mollusc on the planet; while native to Aotearoa New Zealand, it has recently invaded many parts of the world. It is highly variable in shape and size, with generally smooth and small shells occurring in mossy seepages and ditches, but with much larger specimens found in rivers and lakes, often with a spiral row of short regular black spines. In Aotearoa this snail reproduces sexually, but in areas it has invaded it reproduces asexually when it faces less pressure from parasites. Many similar species occur around Aotearoa.

## DECAPITATED WATER SNAIL
*Zemelanopsis trifasciata*

**Distribution:** Both main islands. Lives in coastal freshwater habitats.

**Size:** Shell height to 36mm.

The decapitated water snail lives in slightly brackish water near river mouths. The common name stems from the fact that in abrasive or acidic water conditions the apex of the shell is often broken or eroded away, giving the shell a 'decapitated' look. These snails often appear black, especially at maturity; smaller individuals, or those with no precipitate build-up, are olive-green with brown bands.

## LUMINOUS LIMPET
*Latia neritoides*

**Distribution:** Te Ika-a-Maui North Island. Usually lives attached to rocks in shaded areas in streams.

**Size:** Shell length to 11mm.

Luminous limpets often appear black due to a thin mineral coating on their shells. They are most commonly encountered in shaded streams and are rare in rivers or lakes. Inside the shell, a thin spike-like structure helps the animal hold its shell in areas with strong currents. When disturbed, the limpets can emit a blue bioluminescent slime, which is unique among freshwater gastropods.

#### MUHEKE, PŪPŪ-TARAHIKI
## PAPER NAUTILUS
*Argonauta nodosus*

**Distribution:** Worldwide in tropical and temperate seas. Lives free-swimming in coastal waters.

**Size:** Shell diameter to 248mm (female only).

The female paper nautilus makes a large and delicate shell to protect her egg cases. Paper nautiluses are a species of octopus that live in free-swimming schools. Shells are most often found on small islands. A similar, rarer species, *Argonauta argo*, occurs in Te Ika-a-Māui North Island, and differs in having long ripple-like sculpture on the shell, rather than numerous nodules.

#### KOTAKOTA NGŪ
## RAM'S HORN SHELL
*Spirula spirula*

**Distribution:** Worldwide in tropical and temperate seas. Pelagic.

**Size:** Shell diameter to 20mm.

The ram's horn shell is highly distinctive. It is formed by a small species of squid as a means of regulating buoyancy. Because the shells are positively buoyant, when the squid die their shells float up to the surface and drift with the wind and currents. These shells can often be found in large numbers on exposed beaches.

# GLOSSARY
# REFERENCES
# ACKNOWLEDGEMENTS

# GLOSSARY

**Beak**  The oldest part of a bivalve shell.

**Benthic**  Living on the sea floor.

**Bioluminescence**  The phenomenon where living organisms produce light. Some complex organisms produce light themselves, while others host bioluminescent bacteria to produce light.

**Bivalve**  Member of a mollusc class (Bivalvia) that includes clams, oysters, mussels, scallops, cockles, and others. Bivalves generally have two shells (bi = two, valve = shell).

**Bryozoan**  A phylum that includes many encrusting or coral-like habitat-forming species. Also called lace-corals.

**Byssal thread**  A hair-like structure created by some bivalves to attach to the substrate.

**Cephalopod**  Member of the mollusc class Cephalopoda, which includes squid, octopus, nautilus, cuttlefish, and others.

**Chemosymbiotic**  Chemosymbiotic species host chemosynthetic bacteria (bacteria that can metabolise hydrogen sulphide, methane or carbon dioxide), from which they partially or fully derive their nutrition.

**Chiton**  Chiton species have eight wing-shaped shells enclosed within a leathery girdle. They form the mollusc class Polyplacophora.

**Class**  A taxonomic rank used to classify species with a shared evolutionary history.

**Columella**  The central structural core of the spiral part of a gastropod shell.

**Cord**  A raised, rounded ridge or rib on a shell.

**Denticle**  A raised hump or rib in the aperture of a gastropod.

**Endemic**  A species that is endemic to a region is found nowhere else.

**Epifauna**  Species that live above the sediments (antonym: infauna).

**Filter-feeder**  Species that feed by filtering food particles and/or plankton out of the water.

**Gastropod**  Member of the mollusc class Gastropoda, which includes slugs, snails, limpets, nudibranchs, conches, whelks, and others.

**Girdle**  The leathery or scaly area of a chiton.

**Intertidal zone** The area on the seashore between the high-tide and low-tide zones.

**Keel** A spiral ridge.

**Lamellae** Thin ridges.

**Nacre** A pearly form of calcium carbonate.

**Operculum** A trapdoor-like structure produced by gastropods, which can fully or partially seal the aperture when the body is retracted into the shell.

**Pelagic** Living in the water above the sea floor.

**Periostracum** A thin outer shell layer, usually comprised of chitin.

**Protozoan** A member of a group of small single-celled animals.

**Radula** A feeding structure comprising rows of teeth arranged along a membrane.

**Sculpture** Surface ornamentation.

**Sessile** Sessile organisms attach to the sea floor or other substrates and are generally not independently mobile.

**Shell** A carbonate structure produced by invertebrates. Some authors would limit this definition to exclude structures such as corals.

**Siphon** A tubular structure made of fleshy tissue or shell.

**Siphonal notch** A groove in the outer lip.

**Striation** Narrow groove.

**Sublittoral** Living below low-tide level.

**Substrate** The surface on which an organism lives, or to which it is attached.

**Symbiotic** Where two or more species work together to mutual benefit.

**Tusk shell** Member of the mollusc class Scaphopoda.

**Umbilicus** A concavity on the underside of some gastropod species.

**Valve** A shell from a bivalve or chiton.

**Varix** A large rib.

**Ventral** The underside of an object (antonym: dorsal).

# REFERENCES

Carson, S and R Morris, *The New Zealand Seashore Guide*, Potton & Burton, Nelson, 2022.

Willan, RC, S de C Cook, HG Spencer, RG Creese, S O'Shea and GD Jackson, 'Phylum Mollusca', in: Cook, S de C (ed.), *New Zealand Coastal Marine Invertebrates*, Vol. 1, Canterbury University Press, Christchurch, 2010, pp. 296–566.

# ACKNOWLEDGEMENTS

We would like to acknowledge and thank Jo Elliott and Michael Upchurch at Te Papa Press for driving this project, and Jean-Claude Stahl for his extraordinary photographs.

Thanks also to Teresa McIntyre for the copy edit, Caren Wilton and Mike Wagg for the proof-reads, Sarah Elworthy for typesetting, Yoan Jolly for image preparation, and Tim Denee for the cover and series design.

# INDEX OF SPECIES

Bold page numbers refer to species descriptions.

## A
Aiwhatiwhati **37**
*Alcithoe*
    *arabica* **109**
    *fusus* **109**
*Amalda*
    *australis* **111**
    *depressa* **111**
    *mucronate* **111**
    *northlandica* 109
    *novaezelandiae* **109**
*Amphibola crenata* **115**
Anga nui niho **117**
Angarite **35**
Angel wing **55**
Angled wedge shell **39**
*Anomia trigonopsis* **29**
*Antalis nana* **55**
Arabic volute **109**
*Argobuccinum*
    *pustulosum* **93**
*Argonauta*
    *argo* 125
    *nodosus* **125**
Arid top shell **65**
Ark shell **21**
*Arthritica crassiformis* 55
*Astraea heliotropium* **73**
Ataata, Atāta **73**
*Atalacmea fragilis* **77**
*Atrina zelandica* **21**
*Aulacomya maoriana* **23**
Australasian triton **91**
*Austrofusus glans* **99**
*Austrolittorina*
    *antipodum* **75**
    *cincta* **75**
*Austrovenus*
    *stutchburyi* **47**
Awanui **91**

## B
Banded ear shell **117**
*Barbatia*
    *novaezelandiae* **21**
*Barnea similis* **55**
*Bartschicoma gaimardi* **39**
Basket shell **55**
*Bassina yatei* **49**
*Benhamina obliquata* **117**

Black horn shell **87**
Black mussel **25**
Black nerite **75**
Black top shell **65**
Black-foot pāua **57**
Blue mussel **23**
Blue periwinkle **75**
Bluff oyster **31**
Box shell **29**
Brown bubble shell **115**
Brown mussel **25**
Brown olive **111**
Brown periwinkle **75**
*Buccinulum*
    *linea* **97**
    *vittatum* **97**
*Bulla*
    *quoyii* **115**
    *vernicosa* 115
    *vernicosa* 115
Butterfly chiton **19**
Butterfly shell 39

## C
*Cabestana*
    *spengleri* **93**
    *tabulata* **93**
*Cantharidus opalus* 8, **61**
Cask shell **91**
Cat's eye **73**
*Cellana*
    *denticulate* **79**
    *ornate* **77**
    *radians* **79**
    *stellifera* **79**
    *strigilis* **79**
*Charonia*
    *lampas* **91**
    *tritonis* **91**
*Charopa coma* **119**
*Chiton glaucus* **19**
Circular saw shell **73**
*Cirsotrema zelebori* **95**
Coarse biscuit clam **45**
Coarse dosinia **45**
Cockle **47**
*Coelotrochus*
    *tiaratus* **61**
    *viridis* **61**

*Cominella*
    *adspersa* **99**
    *glandiformis* **101**
    *maculosa* **99**
    *quoyana* **101**
    *virgata* **101**
Common auger **113**
Common charopa
    snail **119**
Common fan scallop **33**
Common myadora **29**
Common tower shell **81**
Common trophon **105**
Convex slipper shell **83**
Cook's turban **73**
*Cookia sulcate* **73**
*Corbula zelandica* **55**
*Crassula aequilatera* **41**
*Cryptoconchus porosus* **19**

## D
Dark olive **111**
Dark rock shell **103**
Dark top shell **65**
Decapitated water
    snail **123**
Deep burrower **43**
Denticulate limpet **79**
Depressed olive **111**
*Dicathais orbita* **107**
*Diloma*
    *aethiops* **63**
    *aridum* **65**
    *bicanaliculatum* **63**,
      65
    *coracina* 65
    *durvillaea* 65
    *nigerrimum* **65**
    *subrostratum* **63**
    *zelandicum* **65**
*Divalucina cumingi* **35**
*Dosina mactracea* **47**
*Dosinia*
    *anus* **45**
    *lambata* 45
    *maoriana* **45**
    *subrosea* **45**
Dredge oyster **31**
Duck's bill shell **59**
*Duplicaria tristis* **113**
Dwarf olive **109**

**E**
*Echyridella*
 *aucklandica* 119
 *menziesii* 119
Elegant limpet 59
Elegant venus shell 51
*Emarginula striatula* 59
Encrusted limpet 77

**F**
Fine biscuit clam 45
Fine dosinia 45
Fine fan scallop 33
Fingerprint limpet 77
Flat oyster 31
Flax snail 119
Fragile bubble shell 115
Fragile limpet 77
Freshwater mussel 119
Freshwater snail 11, 123
Frilled venus shell 49

**G**
*Gari*
 *convexa* 53
 *lineolate* 53
 *stangeri* 53
Geoduck 43
Globose violet snail 95
*Glycymeris modesta* 27
Golden jingle shell 29
Grant's tiger shell 71
Green chiton 19
Green top shell 61
Green window oyster 29
Green-lipped mussel 23

**H**
Hahari 45, 49
Hairy slipper shell 85
Hairy triton 93
Hākari 45, 49
*Haliotis*
 *iris* 57
 *virginea* 57
Hānea 25
Hanikura, Hanikura-patu 39
Harihari 45, 49
*Haustrum*
 *albomarginatum* 103
 *haustorium* 103
 *scobina* 103
Helmet shell 89
*Herpetopoma bellum* 69
*Hiatula*
 *nitida* 51
 *siliquens* 51

Hinangi 47
Hochstetter's snail 121
Hoemoana 21
Hopetea 107
Horse mussel 21
Hūai 47
Huamutu 97
Huangi, Hūangiangi, Hūngungi 47
Hururoa 21
Hutton's top shell 67
Hūwai 47

**I**
*Irus*
 *elegans* 51
 *reflexus* 51
*Ischnochiton maorianus* 19

**J**
*Janthina*
 *exigua* 95
 *globosa* 95
 *janthina* 95
 *umbilicata* 95

**K**
Kāeo 73, 103
Kahitua 37
Kaikai tio 103
Kaikaikaroro 41, 49
Kaikai-karoro 89
Kaitangata 73
Kaitua 37
Kākahi 35, 119
Kākara 73, 99, 103
Kākihi awaawa 117
Kākihi 77, 79, 117
Kaokaoroa 19
Karahū, Karahue 115
Kararuri 57
Karauria 31
Karehu 115
Karoro 49
Kauri snail 121
Kawari 99, 101
Knobbed top shell 63
Knobbed whelk 99
Koeti 87
Koio 57
Kōkota 35
Kōmore 55
Kōrama 73
Koriakai 115
Korona 25
Kota 69
Kotakota ngū 125
Kotakota 35

Kōwhā 47
Kua kua 27
Kuakua 33
Kuhakuha 27
Kuhara, Kuharu 53
Kuku 23
Kūkuku, Kūkukuroa 21
Kukukuroaroa 81
Kuku-mau-toka 25
Kukupara 25
Kukupati, Kupa, Kūpā 21
Kūtai 23
Kute 21
Kuwharu 53

**L**
Lace cockle 35
*Lamellitrophon*
 *traversi* 105
Lance mactra 43
Large dog cockle 27
Large ostrich foot 89
Large siphon limpet 117
Large trophon 105
Large trough shell 41
Large trumpet 91
Large venus shell 47
Large violet snail 95
Large wedge shell 39
*Latia neritoides* 123
*Leukoma crassicosta* 49
Lined limpet 77
Lined tower shell 81
Lined whelk 97
*Linucula hartvigiana* 27
Luminous limpet 123
*Lunella smaragda* 73

**M**
*Macomona liliana* 39
*Mactra*
 *discors* 41
 *murchisoni* 41
*Magallana gigas* 31
Māihi 63, 65
*Maoricolpus roseus* 81
*Maoricrypta*
 *costata* 83
 *monoxyla* 83
 *sodalist* 83
 *youngi* 83
*Maorimactra ordinaria* 41
*Maoristylus*
 *ambagiosus* 119
 *hongi* 119
Marapeka 57
Matangārahu 75
Mātangata 73

Matangongore **61**, **71**
Matapura **75**
*Maurea*
  *granti* **71**
  *punctulate* **71**
  *selecta* **71**
  *tigris* **71**
*Micrelenchus*
  *burchorum* **69**
  *dilatatus* **67**
  *huttonii* **67**
  *purpureus* **69**
  *sanguineus* **67**
  *tenebrosus* **67**
  *tessellatus* **67**
Mimiti, Mitimiti **61**
*Modiolus areolatus* **25**
Moeone **37**
*Monia zelandica* **29**
*Monoplex parthenopeus* **93**
Morning star **47**
Mudflat horn shell **87**
Mudflat snail **115**
Mudflat top shell **63**
Mudflat whelk **101**
Muheke **125**
*Murexsul octogonus* **107**
*Musculus impactus* **25**
*Myadora striata* **29**
*Mytilus planulatus* **23**

**N**
Necklace shell **87**
*Nerita melanotragus* **75**
Nesting mussel **25**
New Zealand
  gooey duck **43**
  *moon snail* **87**
  *mud snail* **123**
  *pen shell* **21**
  *scallop* **33**
  *tower shell* **113**
  *worm shell* **85**
Ngāeo **73**, **103**
Ngaeti **75**
Ngaingai **35**
Ngākihi awaawa **117**
Ngākihi kopia **85**
Ngākihi **31**, **83**, **117**
Ngakihi **77**, **79**
Ngārahu-tatawa, Ngārahu-taua, Ngārura,
  Ngāruru **73**
Niania **25**
Northern lined whelk **97**
Nut shell **27**

**O**
Oblong venus shell **49**
Octagonal murex **107**
*Onithochiton neglectus* **19**
Opal top shell **8**, **61**
Orange-mouthed
  whelk **101**
Ornate limpet **77**
*Ostrea chilensis* **31**
Oyster borer **103**

**P**
Pacific oyster **31**
Pakira **29**
*Panopea zelandica* **43**
Papatai **81**
Papatua **19**
*Papawera zelandiae* **115**
Paper nautilus **125**
*Paphies*
  *australis* **35**
  *donacina* **37**
  *subtriangulata* **37**
  *ventricose* **37**
*Paryphanta busbyi* **121**
*Patelloida corticate* **77**
Pati, Patikuku **21**
Pātiotio **55**
Pāua **57**
Peanut shell **55**
*Pecten novaezelandiae* **33**
Peke **75**
*Pelicaria vermis* **89**
Peraro **43**
*Perna canaliculus* **23**
*Phenatoma*
  *roseum* **113**
  *zealandi* **113**
Pink opal top shell **69**
Pink sunset shell **53**
Pink top shell **69**
Pipi roa **43**
Pipi tairaki **37**
Pipi **35**, **47**
Pipi-kōmore, Pipi-taiari **55**
Pipi-tairaki **37**
Piritoka **117**
*Pleuroloba costellaris* **117**
*Poirieria zelandica* **107**
Poro **29**
Pōrohe **23**
*Potamopyrgus*
  *antipodarum* **11**, **123**
*Powelliphanta*
  *hochstetteri* **9**, **121**
*Pseudarcopagia*
  *disculus* **39**

Puhauriroa **109**
Pukanikani,
  Pūkanikani **23**
Pūkauri **49**
Pukira **29**
Pūpū piatāta **111**
Pūpū rore **109**
Pūpū tuatea **115**
Pūpū waharoa **115**
Pūpū **63**, **73**
Pūpū-atamanama, Pūpū-
  atamarama **73**
Pūpūkarekawa, Pūpū-
  karekawa **73**
Pūpū-kōrama **73**
Pūpū-mai **63**
Pūpūrangi **121**
Pūpū-rore **109**, **111**
Pūpū-tara **91**
Pūpū-tarahiki **125**
Pūpū-tatara **91**
Pūpū-waharoa **115**
Pūpūwhakarongotaua **119**
Purewha **25**
Pūrimu **35**
Purple cockle **35**
Purple sunset shell **51**
*Purpurocardia*
  *purpurata* **35**
Pūtara, Pūtaratara,
  Pūtātara **91**

**Q**
Queen scallop **33**
Quoy's whelk **101**

**R**
Ram's horn shell **125**
*Ranella Australasia* **91**
Rayed sunset shell **53**
Razor mussel **21**
Rehoreho **71**
Repe **31**
Rerekākā **73**
*Resania lanceolata* **43**
Ribbed mussel **23**
Ribbed slipper shell **83**
Ribbed venus shell **49**
Rock borer **55**
Rock oyster **31**
Rori **59**
Roroa **37**, **43**
Rosy tower shell **113**
Rough oyster borer **103**
Rough venus shell **51**
Round wedge shell **39**
Rūharu **77**

**S**
*Saccostrea glomerata* **31**
Scimitar mactra **43**
*Scutus breviculus* **59**
Select tiger shell **71**
*Semicassis*
  *labiata* **89**
  *pyrum* **89**
Shield shell **59**
*Sigapatella*
  *novaezelandiae* **85**
  *tenuis* **85**
*Siphonaria*
  *australis* **117**
  *propria* **117**
Slit limpet **59**
Small dog cockle **27**
Small dosinia **45**
Small opal top shell **67**
Small ostrich foot **89**
Small siphon limpet **117**
Small slipper shell **85**
Small tower shell **81**
Small violet snail **95**
Small volute **109**
Smooth slipper shell **83**
Snakeskin chiton **19**
*Solemya parkinsonii* **21**
Southern olive **111**
Southern tuatua **37**
Speckled whelk **99**
Spengler's trumpet **93**
Spiny murex **107**
*Spirula spirula* **125**
Spotted tiger shell **71**
Spotted top shell **63**
Spotted whelk **99**
Star limpet **79**
Stepped top shell **61**
*Stiracolpus pagoda* **81**
Stout sunset shell **53**
*Struthiolaria papulose* **89**
Swollen triton **93**
*Sypharochiton*
  *pelliserpentis* **19**
  *sinclairi* **19**

**T**
Tai awa, Taiawa **35**
Tairaki, Taiwhatiwhati **37**
Takai, Tākai **89**
Takarepe, Takarepo **53**
Takarepu **115**
Tākupu **109**
*Talochlamys*
  *gemmulata* **33**
  *zelandiae* **33**

*Tanea zelandica* **87**
Tanetane **47**
Taore **23**
Taron **97**
*Taron dubius* **97**
Tātara **91**
Tātoko **115**
*Tawera spissa* **47**
Tāwera **47**
Tawiri **107**
Te ouara **111**
Tessellated top shell **67**
Tetere moana **55**
*Thylacodes zelandicus* **85**
Tiara top shell **61**
Tiger shell **71**
Tihipu **61**
Tikoaka **109, 111**
Tio **31**
Tio para **31**
Tio paruparu **31**
Tio pohatu, Tio repe,
  Tio reperepe, Tiokohatu,
  Tiopara, Tiorepe **31**
Tipa, Tipai **33**
Titoko **115**
Toheroa **37**
Toitoi **73**
*Tonna tankervillii* **91**
Toothed top shell **69**
Toretore **21, 23**
Toritori **23**
Tortoiseshell limpet **79**
Totorere **89**
Travers' murex **105**
Triangle shell **41**
Trough shell **41**
Tua **37**
Tuaki **47, 49**
Tuangi haruru **45**
Tuangi **47, 49**
Tuatua **37**
*Tucetona laticostata* **27**
*Tugali*
  *elegans* **59**
  *suteri* **59**
Tun shell **91**
Tungangi **47**
Tupa **33**
Tupehokura **37**
Tūpere **77**
Tūroro **21**
Tusk shell **55**
Tūteure **91**

**U**
Uere **109, 111**
Ururoa **53**

**V**
*Venerupis largillierti* **49**
Virgin pāua **57**

**W**
Waharoa **21**
Wahawaha **53**
*Wainuia urnula* **121**
Wainuia **121**
Wentletrap **95**
Wētiwha **115**
Wheel shell **69**
Whētiko **63, 115**
Whētikotiko **115**
White bubble shell **115**
White rock shell **107**

**X**
*Xenostrobus*
  *neozelanicus* **25**
  *securis* **25**
*Xymene plebeius* **105**

**Y**
Yellow window oyster **29**

**Z**
*Zeacolpus vittatus* **81**
*Zeacumantus*
  *lutulentus* **87**
  *subcarinatus* **87**
*Zeatrophon*
  *ambiguous* **105**
*Zemelanopsis*
  *trifasciata* **123**
*Zenatia acinaces* **43**
*Zethalia zelandica* **69**

# ABOUT THE AUTHORS

Dr Bruce Marshall is a malacologist who has worked at Te Papa, and the previous National Museum, since 1976. He has collected aquatic life since childhood, at 11 creating his first formal collection, which comprised mostly marine and fossil shells self-collected from near his home in the eastern Bay of Plenty. As museum collection manager of molluscs, Bruce was responsible for the development of a vast collection of several million specimens representing more than 4700 New Zealand species, with special emphasis on the minute forms that comprise the bulk of the phylum Mollusca. His research interests include faunas of decaying wood, algae, fish bones and whale carcasses, various groups of marine, land and freshwater species, and biogeographical relationships within the Aotearoa New Zealand region and between it and the wider western Pacific. He has published over 160 papers in refereed journals and has named over 600 new species and genera of molluscs, as well as several families and subfamilies. Bruce is on the editorial boards of four leading international journals on Mollusca, has edited several volumes of the series *Tropical Deep-Sea Benthos*, and is a senior Mollusca editor for MolluscaBase/World Register of Marine Species.

Kerry Walton is an invertebrate curator at Te Papa. His research focuses on understanding the distributions of mollusc species, how these species differ, and how their differences came to be through evolution and dispersal. Kerry is especially interested in the conservation of large land snails and research into unusual deep-sea habitats, such as hydrothermal vents and organic falls. He has experience collaborating on a range of palaeogenetics, conservation, biosecurity and iwi-led projects, and enjoys the opportunities for fieldwork and community engagement that this work brings. His recent work has pioneered new palaeogenetic methods enabling researchers to sequence DNA from shells that are thousands of years old.

First published in New Zealand in 2023 by
Te Papa Press, PO Box 467, Wellington, New Zealand
www.tepapapress.co.nz

Text: Bruce Marshall and Kerry Walton
© Museum of New Zealand Te Papa Tongarewa

All images created by Yoan Jolly from high-resolution
photographs of Te Papa specimens by Dr Jean-Claude Stahl,
except those on page 18, which are by Kerry Walton,
© Museum of New Zealand Te Papa Tongarewa and
the Hochstetter's snail on page 120 (centre), which is
© Kerry Walton.

This book is copyright. Apart from any fair dealing for the
purpose of private study, research, criticism,
or review, as permitted under the Copyright Act, no part of
this book may be reproduced by any process, stored
in a retrieval system, or transmitted in any form, without the
prior permission of the Museum of New Zealand
Te Papa Tongarewa.

TE PAPA® is the trademark of the Museum of
New Zealand Te Papa Tongarewa
Te Papa Press is an imprint of the Museum of
New Zealand Te Papa Tongarewa

A catalogue record is available from the National Library
of New Zealand

978-1-99-116553-4

Cover and internal design by Tim Denee
Cover illustration based on the New Zealand or Queen scallop
(*Pecten novaezelandiae*).
Typesetting by Sarah Elworthy
Digital imaging by Yoan Jolly

Printed by Everbest Printing Investment Limited